The Marriage License Bonds

of

Mecklenburg County, Virginia

from

1765 to 1810

Listed and Indexed by

Stratton Nottingham

CLEARFIELD

Originally Published
[Onancock, Virginia, 1928]

Reprinted
Genealogical Publishing Co., Inc.
Baltimore, 1978

Reprinted for
Clearfield Company, Inc. by
Genealogical Publishing Co., Inc.
Baltimore, Maryland
1992, 1993, 1996, 2003

International Standard Book Number: 0-8063-4639-6

Made in the United States of America

THE MARRIAGE LICENSE BONDS
OF
MECKLENBURG COUNTY, VIRGINIA
1765-1810

"The Marriage License Bonds of Mecklenburg County,
Virginia, 1765 to 1810" is the fourth volume of Virginia
marriages published by the compiler from the loose papers
filed in the County Clerk's Offices.

This volume contains the only official record of
nearly two thousand marriages from Mecklenburg County. There
was no marriage register prior to 1850, and these loose papers
are the only record of hundreds of marriages of vital importance to those interested in Virginia genealogy.

Every item of importance has been abstracted, names
of the contracting parties, dates, place of residence, when
given, sureties &c. The bond itself rarely gives the names
of the parents, but frequently notes were addressed to the
Clerk by the parents authorizing him to issue the license.
Many of these notes are on file with the bonds, and these
have also been noted.

These bonds were abstracted by Mr. John Y. Hutcheson,
Attorney, of Boydton, Va., who is thoroughly familiar with the
records of his county, and to whom the compiler wishes to
acknowledge his sincere appreciation, as it was through the
courtesy of Mr. Hutcheson that he was able to obtain the
abstracts and to list and index them for publication.

Abernathy, Tignal & Martha Holmes, 9 May, 1806, John Harris sec.

Adams, Isaac & Judith Carroll, 30 Dec. 1786, William Parrish sec.
Adams, Jeremiah & Jinsey Redding, 22 Sept. 1798, Drury Creedle sec.
Adams, Richard & Sally Allen, 28 Oct. 1808, Fielding Noel sec.
Adams, Sackfeild & _____ Daly, 23 June, 1795, William Dailey sec.

Adkinson, Arthur C. & Elizabeth Person, 12 Sept. 1791, Thomas Person
    sec.

Akin, Joseph & Mary Eastland, 10 Oct. 1774, William Wastland sec.

Aldridge, John & Agness Baugh, 20 Jan. 1800, E. Macgowan sec.

Alexander, Mark & Lucy Bugg, 20 May 1789, Sam Goode sec.
Alexander, Mark & Elizabeth Q. Mcharg, 19 Jan. 1797, Robert Basker-
    ville sec.
Alexander, Mark & Nancy Eaton, 18 Oct. 1804, William Baskerville sec.

Allen, Arva & Polly Clarke, 1 Aug. 1786, Bolling Clarke sec.
Allen, Charles & Sarah Smith, dau. Drury Smith, 20 Apr. 1781, David
    Royster sec.
Allen, Darling & Judith Nance, 9 May, 1783, Robert Nance sec.
Allen, Ephraim & Patsey Skelton, 13 Feb. 1792, Thomas Allen sec.
Allen, Gray & Molley Nance, 16 Dec. 1791, William Drumright sec.
    Notes from grooms brother Darling Allen, wit. Stacy Drum-
    right & bride's father, Robert Nance, wit. Drury Allen.
Allen, James & Frances Conner, 13 Apr. 1795, Burwell Russell sec.
Allen, John & Nancy Morgain, 15 Dec. 1783, Frederick Rainey sec.
Allen, John, of Buckingham Co., & Elizabeth Bugg, 3 Oct. 1791,
    Thomas Langley sec.
Allen, John & Patsey Cox, 14 Jan. 1793, Thomas Cox sec.
Allen, John & Martha Colley, 12 Nov. 1798, William Brown sec.
Allen, John & Constant Merriott, 3 Mar. 1806, Thos.Merriott sec.
Allen, Jones & Nancy Lewis, 8 Jan. 1810, Robert Lewis sec.
Allen, Mariday, son of William Allen, & Nancy Cooper, 9 Aug. 1788,
    John Bailey sec.
Allen, Matthews & Mary Brawner, 8 May 1797, James Thompson sec.
Allen, Pleasant & Rebeccah Watson, 8 Aug. 1787, John Allen sec.
    Note signed Robekah & Wm. Allen, Senr.
Allen, Richard M. & Elizabeth B. Blacketter, 6 Nov. 1809, David
    Blacketter sec.
Allen, Robert Jones & Caty Hollins, 1 Dec. 1786, Thomas Richardson
    sec.
Allen, Ruel & Mary Pulliam, 13 Jan. 1794, James Norment sec.
Allen, Thomas & Lucy Adams, 13 Dec. 1796, John Freeman sec.
Allen, Young & Sarah Poole, 27 Feb. 1786, Darling Allen sec.

Allgood, Edward & Elizabeth Hudson, 28 Nov. 1788, Bartlett Cox sec.
Allgood, George & Dicy Hudson, 23 Jan. 1806, Thomas Mallett sec.
Allgood, Jermiah & Dice Harris, 13 Dec. 1802, James Harris sec.
Allgood, John & Jinsey Blake, 31 Dec. 1798, Edward Goodrich sec.
Allgood, Samuel & Mary Royal, 4 Oct. 1786, Edward Clarke sec.
Allgood, Samuel & Jinny Claunch, 29 Dec. 1804, Matthew Claunch sec.
Allgood, William & Sarah Royal, 5 Mar. 1790, Manly Allgood sec.

Alston, John & Jane H. Davis, 14 Dec. 1799, Thomas H. Davis sec.

Andrews, Ephriam & Stacy Humphress, 15 Feb. 1786, Thomas Humphress sec.
Andrews, Thomas & Margaret Broadfoot, 29 Mar. 1791, Frederick Andrews sec.

Anderson, Charles, of Amelia Co., & Salley Thornton, 11 Sept. 1787, James Thornton sec.
Anderson, Jordan, of Prince Edward Co., & Margaret Easter, 6 June, 1785, Lewis Rolfe sec.
Anderson, Joseph & Martha Edmondson, 12 Aug. 1794, William Phillips sec.

Apperson, David & Martha Speed, 13 May, 1778, Richard Hanserd sec.
Apperson, Samuel & Polly Worsham, 1 Oct. 1801, Archibald Clarke sec.
    Note from bride's father, John Worsham, wit: John Gregory.
Apperson, Thomas & Kitty Wynn, 6 Aug. 1791, Holeman Rui sec.

Armistead, John & Elizabeth Royster, dau. William Royster, 17 July, 1777, John Farrar sec. Note of William Royster wit. by John & Seymour Puryear.

Arnold, Isaac & Ann Andrews, 16 May, 1795, George Hightower Walker sec.
Arnold, Joseph & Frances Drumright, 24 Sept. 1800, William Drumright sec.

Ashton, Henry & Elizabeth Hanner Barbary Watts, 31 Mar. 1788, Richard Watt sec.

Atkins, Thomas & Sally Johnston, 8 Jan. 1810, Caleb Johnston sec.

Avory (Avery), Brown & Elizabeth Royster, 27 Jan. 1810, Miles Hall sec.
Avory (Evars), Elijah & Delia Crew, 12 June 1809, Leeman Haile sec.
Avory, James & Polly Spain, 12 Dec. 1808, Abraham Reamy sec.
Avory, Jarrotte & Rebecca Worsham, 17 Dec. 1810, Daniel Jones sec.
Avery, Joel & Franky Puryear, 12 Dec. 1808, Elijah Puryear sec.
Avery, Matthew & Obedience Crowder, 12 Sept. 1803, John Wagstaff sec.

Averett, Thomas & Rebecca Allen, 13 July, 1807, Joel Allen sec.

Bagwell, Samuel, of Brunswick Co. & Catherine Brown, 12 Nov. 1788, Richard Edmondson sec.

Bailey (Bayley), Benjamin & Patsey Durham, 11 June 1798, Valentine McCutcheon sec.
Bailey, George & Duamar Hicks, 21 Oct. 1799, Bartholomew Medley sec.
Bailey, Henry & Polley Edwards, 9 Dec. 1793, Thomas Edwards sec.
    Note from John Edwards, father of Polley.
Bailey, Henry & Jessie Curtis, 17 Feb. 1802, Jesse Curtis sec.

Bailey, Howard & Elizabeth Vaughan, 3 Dec. 1783, John Bell sec.
Bailey, John & Anne Allen, 2 Mar. 1791, Elisha Arnold sec.
Bailey, Peter & Sarah Baker, 27 Aug. 1793, Thomas Jeffress sec.
Bailey, William & Martha Holloway, 21 Nov. 1801, Henry Bailey sec.

Baird, Charles W. & Fanny D. Gregory, 6 Dec. 1808, West Gregory sec.
Baird, John & Salley Cunningham, 3 May 1805, Jesse Johnson sec.

Baker, James & Polly Holmes, 4 Oct. 1809, Richard Crowder sec.
Baker, William & Leah Hendrick, 12 May 1800, George Baker sec.

Baptist, Matthew & Aphia W. Clausel, 11 Dec. 1809, Benjamin W. Jeffries sec.

Barber, Edward & Jincey Williamson, 9 Dec. 1799, James Greenwood sec. Note from Robert Williamson, father of Jincey

Barker, Charles, of Nottoway Co. & Barbary Wootton, 15 Aug. 1791, John Wootton sec.

Barnor, Harrison & Polly Jones, 17 May, 1786, Theophilus Harrison sec.

Barnes, Brackett & Jane Jeffries, 8 May, 1797, Swepson Jeffries sec.
Barnes, John, of Brunswick Co. & Rebecca Winkfield, 15 Jan. 1794, Joshua Winfeld sec.
Barnes, Phillip & Mary White, 8 Jan. 1798, William Naish sec.

Barron, John & Charlotte Watson, 2 Dec. 1809, James Standley sec.

Barrow, William & Susannah Marshall, 2 May 1801, Dennis Marshall sec.

Barnett, John & Salley Merryman, 7 Aug. 1805, Richard Hailey sec.
Barnet, Thomas & Hannah Book, 10 June, 1790, William Walker sec.
Barnet, William & Judith Thomason, 10 Jan. 1793, William Bowen sec.

Barry, James H. & Patsey Thompson, 20 Jan. 1808, William Crow sec.
Barry, Joseph & Mary Massey, 30 Dec. 1795, Drury Andrews sec. Note from Thomas & Mary Massey, parents of bride - wit. by Mary Barry

Baskervill, Edward & Susannah Holmes, 4 Mar. 1800, John Dortch sec.
Baskervill, George H. & Elizabeth Tabb, 16 Dec. 1791, Robert Baskervill sec.
Baskervill, John & Martha Burton, 30 July 1765, Samuel Young sec.

Basey, Jesse & Jane Perrin Giles, 19 Dec. 1791, Isham Eppes sec.

Baugh, Daniel & Lucy Brooks, spinster, 10 Oct. 1780, John Eppes sec.
Baugh, James & Peggy Smith, dau. John Smith, 22 Dec. 1800, John Smith, Jr. sec.
Baugh, Richard & Elizabeth P. Harwell, 28 May, 1800, Edward Patrick Davis sec. Note from Jas.Harwell, father of Eliza-

beth - wit. by Lucy Marable
Baugh, William B. & Martha Minge Bilbo, 15 Nov. 1804,Wm.Baskervill sec.
Bayley (Bailey), Richard & Anne Brown, 12 Jan. 1795, William Brown
    sec.

Beauford, Daniel & Sarah Hightower, 24 Mar. 1787, Thomas Jones sec.

Beasley, James & Rebecca Jones, 10 Sept. 1800, Uriah Hawkins sec.
Beasley, John & Martha N. Insco, 15 June 1801, William Insco sec.
Beasley, Thomas & Salley Jackson, 22 Dec. 1800, Mark L. Jackson sec.
Beasley, William & Rebecca Vaughan, 19 May 1804, Reuben Vaughan sec.

Beaver, William & Elizabeth Hutcheson, 28 Dec. 1789, James Jones sec.

Bedford, James & Frances Maynard, 17 Nov. 1786, William Maynard sec.
Bedford, John, of Charl. Co. & Mary Ann Marshall, 10 Sept. 1787,
    Francis Marshall sec.

Bell, John & Mary Butler, 12 Jan. 1785, William Lucas sec.

Bennett, Anthony & Susanna Davis, 13 Dec. 1779, John Brown sec.
Bennett, Jonathan & Sarah Tanner, 17 Dec. 1793, Thomas Tanner sec.
Bennett, Joseph & Nancy Lanier, 24 May 1785, Ingram Vaughan sec.
Bennett, Joseph & Elizabeth Barnes, 1 Apr. 1787, Anthony Bennet sec.
Bennett, Jordan & Mary Ann Tanner, 14 Mar. 1791, Anthony Bennett
    sec.
Bennett, Jordan & Nancy Murfey, 15 Dec. 1795, Thomas Tanner sec.
Bennett, Matthew & Polley Thompson, 1 Nov. 1800, John Thompson sec.
Bennett, William & Nancy Williams, 13 Feb. 1799, Lewis Williams sec.
Bennett, William & Tabathia Lanier, 1 Oct. 1807, Philip Roberts sec.

Benford, Thomas & Rebekah Thompson, 16 Jan. 1804, Edward Thompson
    sec.

Bevill, Thomas & Nancy Keeton, 24 Jan. 1797, Hutchens Burton sec.
Bevill, William & Nancy Prevett, 22 Dec. 1800, Thomas Johnson sec.

Bilbo, Allen Moss & Martha Farrar, 15 Dec. 1810, Benjamin Whitlow
    sec. Note from John Farrar father of Martha - wit. Henry
    Hicks
Bilbo, John & Mary Clemonds, 28 Sept. 1786, Nicholas Bilbo sec.
Bilbo, John & Mary Nicholson, 2 Apr. 1807, George H. Baskervill
    sec.
Bilbo, Joseph & Jane Greer, 11 Sept. 1780, Zach Bowers sec. Note
    from Joseph Greer, father of Jane - wit. Thomas Greer.

Binford, Thomas & Elizabeth Osling, 25 Dec. 1786, John Osling sec.
    Note from Jesse Osling, father of Elizabeth - wit. John
    Osling, Lewis Williams, Caleb Anderson.
Binford, Thomas & Susanna Finch, 7 May 1795, William Finch sec.

Bird, William & Sylvia Bass, 29 Nov. 1802, Independence Poarch sec.

Bishop, Jeremiah & Elizth Colley, 8 Feb. 1802, Charles Colley sec.

Black, Frederick, of Campbell Co. & Elizabeth Lockett, 11 Jan. 1790,
Royal Lockett sec.
Black, Stephen, of Campbell Co. & Temperance Clay, 8 Jan. 1793,
Britain Clay sec. Note from Charles & Pheby Clay, parents of
Temperance.

Bland, John & Salley Burnett, 22 Apr. 1794, Auselin Bugg sec. Note
from Eliza Burnett, mother of Salley - wit. Thomas Burnett.
Bland, William & Darcus Williams, 17 Nov. 1806, James Bugg sec.

Blackbourn, Clement & Mary Lewis, 21 Oct. 1784, Francis Lewis sec.

Blake, Benjamin & Sally Whobry, 3 Apr. 1809, George B. Hamner sec.

Blacketter, David & Mary F. Cox, 13 Dec. 1796, Edward Cox sec.
Blacketter, William & Elizabeth Allgood, 24 Dec. 1793, Bartlett
Cox sec.

Blanton, Green & Nancy D. Overby, 15 Feb. 1810, Adam Overby sec.

Booker, Jonathan & Lucy Simmons, 10 Aug. 1795, Thomas Jones sec.
Booker, Lowry & Phebe Cox, 11 Dec. 1780, John Clay sec - Note
from John Cox, Sr.
Booker, Reuben & Judy Bowen, 19 June, 1801, Daniel Tucker, Jr. sec.
Booker, William & Martha Bizwell, 14 Jan. 1799, Benj. Bizwell sec.
Booker, William & Polley Finch __ Nov. 1802, John Puryear,Jr. sec.

Booth, John & Salley Read Marshall, 9 Apr. 1805, John Johnson sec.
Note from Richard Marshall, father of Salley Read.
Booth, John & Elizabeth Mabry, 29 Dec. 1810, Edward Giles sec.

Boswell, John & Mary Coleman, 16 Feb. 1784, James Coleman sec.
Note from Clus Coleman, father of Mary.
Boswell, Joseph & Susanna Pettus, 9 Dec. 1805, William Pettue sec.
Note from Samuel Pettus, father of Susanna - wit. William
Pettus.

Bottom, Anderson & Sally Hatchell, 30 May 1809, William H.Bugg sec.
Bottom, Bolling, of Brunswick County & Martha Harper, 14 Mar. 1796,
Wyatt Harper sec.
Bottom, William & Elizabeth Richardson, 20 Dec. 1806, Nathaniel
Moss sec.

Bowen, Asa & Charlotte Bowen, 6 Dec. 1796, Charles Bowen sec.
Bowen, Benjamin & Martha Sparks, 12 Sept. 1803, Zachariah Yancey
sec.
Bowen, Charnel & Omoa Bowen, 15 Oct. 1805, Berry Bowen sec.
Bowen, Elisha & Magdala Salley, 24 Aug. 1803, John Turner, Jr. sec.
Bowen, Hughke & Jiney Finn, 30 Nov. 1801, Littleberry Bowen sec.
Bowen, Jordan & Nancy Pearry, 25 Mar. 1804, John Hudgins sec.
Bowen, Richard Jones & Betsey S. Kirks, 22 Nov. 1808, James Bowen
sec.
Bowen, Zach & Mavel Drummond, 2 Oct. 1795, Thomas Drummond sec.

Bowers, Sanford & Elizabeth Vaughan, 14 Dec. 1790, Richard Edmondson
    sec

Boynton, Elisah S. & Elizabeth Neal, 31 Dec. 1808, James Mealer sec.

Boyd, Alexander & Matilda Burwell, 10 Oct. 1803, John Dortch sec.
    Note from Armistead Burwell, father of Matilda
Boyd, Richard & Panthea Burwell, 19 Nov. 1799, John Wryth sec.
    Note from Lewis Burwell, father of Panthea - wit. Rich'd.
    Swepson & Alex. Boyd, Jr.
Boyd, Robert & Sarah Anderson Jones, 20 Apr. 1789, Major Butler sec.
    Note from Alex Boyd, father of Robert - wit. Jean Young &
    William Boyd - Note from Tignal Jones, father of Sarah -
    wit. Thomas Anderson & William White.

Boyd, Robert & Tabitha Walker, 11 May 1803, John Dortch sec.

Brame, David & Barbara Hester, 28 Nov. 1807, James Hester sec.
Brame, Dickey & Anna Hutcheson, 29 Jan. 1795, Archerbell Phillips
    sec. Note from Richard Hutcheson, father of Anna - wit.
    Richard Hutcheson
Brame, George W. & Dianna Clark, 9 Apr. 1804, Lewis Roffe sec.
Brame, James C. & Elizabeth B. Daly, 9 Sept. 1806, Wm. Daly sec.
Brame, James & Susanna Brame, 23 Oct. 1810, W. L. Brame sec.
Brame, John & Mary Norman, 18 Mar. 1768, William Norment sec.
Brame, John & Lilly Hester, 9 Dec. 1805, Wm. W. V. Clausel sec.
Brame, Joseph & Jane Hester, 10 Mar. 1806, Wm. W. V. Clausel sec.
Brame, Melchizedeck & Salley Bailey, 1 Jan. 1797, William Rowlet sec.
Brame, Samuel & Elizabeth Roffe, 21 Sept. 1802, Ingram Roffe sec.
    Note from James Brame, father of Samuel
Brame, William & Hannah H. Clausel, 12 Dec. 1808, Alexander B.
    Puryear sec.

Brandon, Edward & Elizabeth Chavaus, 10 Mar. 1806, Frederick Irby
    sec.
Bradley, John & Mary Taylor, 16 Nov. 1772, Lewis Speed sec.
Bradley, Joseph & Rebecca Pattillo, 17 Feb. 1794, Solomon Pattillo
    sec.

Bragg, David & Susanna Goodman, ___ Jan. 1797, Bennett Goodman sec.

Briggs, James & Polley Arnold, 10 Feb. 1794, John Arnold sec.

Bridgewater, William & Barbara Hester, 13 July 1792, Wm.Hunley sec.
Bressie,Francis & Sarah Royster, dau.Jos.,13 Apr.1778,Jos.Royster sec.
Brodie, Dr. Edward & Ann N. Haskins, 4 Dec. 1802, John S. Jeffries
    sec.   Note from Christopher Haskins, father of Ann

Browder, Isham, of Halifax Co. & Tabitha Cox, 3 Feb. 1767, John Cox
    sec - Notes from Mary Cox, mother, & John Cox brother of
    Tabitha.
Browder, Thomas & Betsey Bland, 21 July 1796, Jesse Bugg sec.
Browder, William & Nancy Mitchell, 25 Jan. 1808, William Mitchell
    sec.

Brogdon, William & Caty Carter, 31 Aug. 1786, Benjamin Ferrell sec.

Brown (Browne), James & Sarah Hutson, 29 Dec. 1789, James Cox sec.
Brown, Jeremiah & Elizabeth Douglass, 28 Aug. 1770, William Douglass
     sec.
Brown, Jeremiah & Mary Gregory, 10 Nov. 1806, Jesse Craddock sec.
Brown, Jesse & Ann Bolling Murray, 16 Sept. 1786, Sam Goode sec.
     Note from Susanna Murray - wit. Edw. R. & Elizabeth Yates
Browne,Jessie & Patsey Vaughan, 28 May 1789, Thomas Vaughan sec.
Brown, John & Lucy Jeffress, 22 Nov. 1800, William Brown sec.
Brown Pettus & Polly Cluverias Jeffries, 22 Apr. 1809, Thomas Brown
     sec. Note from Mercia Coleman - wit. S. Brown.
Brown, Rich'd & Lucy Hester, 28 Dec. 1801, Littleberry Rudd sec.
Brown, William & Salley Hutcheson, 14 Dec. 1789, Richard Hutcheson
     sec.
Brown, William & Mary Roffe, 10 Mar. 1806, Meleh Roffe sec.

Brooks, Robert Rose (an infant) & Mary Parham, 20 Nov. 1780 -
     Daniel Baugh sec. Note from Robert Brooks, father of Robert
     Rose - wit. Wade Brooks
Brookes, Wade & Tabitha Jones, 7 Jan. 1796, John Webb sec.

Brooking, Robert Edward & Lucy Delony, 9 May 1779, Henry Delony sec.
     Note from V. Brooking - wit. Edw: Brodnax. Note from Henry
     Delony.

Brummit, Leroy & Jane Freeman, 7 Dec. 1800, Benjamin Freeman sec.

Bugg, Benjamin & Anne Andrews, 3 Sept. 1785, Ephriam Andrews, Jr.
     sec. Note from Ephriam Andrews, father of Anne - wit. John
     Young & William Drumright.
Bugg, Benjamin & Tabitha Walden, 3 May 1805, James Noel sec.
Bugg, Edmond & Sarah Jeffries, 10 Dec. 1792, Swepson Jeffries sec.
Bugg, Jacob & Sarah Davis, 27 July 1791, Sherwood Bugg sec.
     Note from father of Sarah Davis signed "J.D."
Bugg, Jacob & Mary Thweate Tucker, 11 Sept. 1798, Benjamin Tucker
     sec.
Bugg, James & Rebecca Pulley, 8 Dec. 1800, Samuel Bugg sec.
Bugg, John & Rebeccah Mitchell, 17 Dec. 1788, James Sandefer sec.
Bugg, Samuel & Elizabeth Bilbo, 25 Mar. 1794, Bennet Sandefer sec.
Bugg, Sherwood & Sarah Speed, 31 Dec. 1787, Joseph Speed sec.
Bugg, William & Lucy Hix, 7 Nov. 1773, Amos Hix sec.
Bugg, William & Fanney Holmes, 22 Jan. 1803, John Holmes, sec.
Bugg, Zacharcah & Mary C. Taylor, 9 Dec. 1803, Roger Gregory sec.

Bullock, William & Elzh Lewis, 20 Aug. 1766, Edmond Taylor sec.

Bullington, John & Bicy Reader, 20 Mar. 1797, John Cox sec. Note
     from Grace Reader, mother of Bicy - wit. James Allen

Burwell, Armistead & Lucy Crawley, 14 Nov. 1791, Robt.Crawley sec.

Burton, Allen & Rebeccah Hambler, 22 Mar. 1786, Isaac Pulley sec.
Burton, Benjamin & Monier Humphries, 19 June 1775, John Hunphries
     sec.

Burton, Charles & Elizabeth Johnston, 9 Sept. 1793, Thos.Wilson sec.
Burton, Charles & Catherine Foster, 11 Aug. 1806, Wm.W. Green sec.
Burton, Charles & Elizabeth Burnes, 9 Nov. 1807, Vinson Garner sec.
Burton, Elisha & Elizabeth Camberlaia, 14 Jan. 1805, Joseph B.
        Clausel sec.
Burton, James & Lambert Cuzzy, 8 Dec. 1792, Mark Lambert Jackson sec.
Burton, John & Clary Vaughan, 20 Feb. 1787, Ambros Vaughan, of Brun-
        swick Co. sec.
Burton, John & Elzth R. Brame, 9 Feb. 1801, Edward Rolfe sec.
Burton, Micajah & Susanna Puryear, 3 July 1791, Robert Burton sec.
Burton, Owen & Mary Hester, 8 Jan. 1798, Robert Marshall sec.
Burton, Robert & Milley Lambert, 9 July 1800, James Burton sec.
Burton, Thomas Haly & Martha Humphries, 30 Sept. 1783, John Hump-
        hries sec.
Burton, William & Molley Brooks, 22 Jan. 1774, William Brooks sec.
Burton, William & Patsey Mitchell, 30 Dec. 1806, Gideon Walker sec.
Burton, William & Jinney Carroll, 12 Apr. 1810, Jonas Burton sec.

Burnett, Edmund & Rebecca Crowder, 31 Oct. 1797, Isaac Arnold sec.
        Note from John Crowder, father of Rebecca.
Burnett, Henry & Milley Crowder, 21 Oct. 1789, John Crowder sec.
Burnett, Robert & Nancy Whoberry, 23 Oct. 1798, William Whoberry
        sec. Note from Jacob Whoberry, father of Nancy - wit.
        Joseph Burnett & John Whoberry.
Burnett, Thomas & Elizabeth Jeffries, 4 Aug. 1785, Geo. H. Basker-
        vill sec. Note from Swepson Jeffries, father of Elizabeth
        wit. T. Vaughan, Ann Lewis.
Burnett, William & Martha Jeffries, 1 Oct. 1794, Swepson Jeffries
        sec. Note from Swepson Jeffries, father of Martha - wit.
        Dan'l. Wilson, Jr.

Burnes, George & Elizth Puryear, 8 Oct. 1804, Hutchens Burton sec.

Burruss, Wiley & Peggy Gordan, 14 Aug. 1809, William Burton sec.

Butler, John O. & Frances C. Hutcheson, 9 Dec. 1804, William Brow-
        der sec.
Butler, John & Nancy Stone, 10 Nov. 1806, Edward Jones sec.
Butler, Joseph & Frances Oliver, 9 June 1783, John Oliver sec.
Butler, Lewis & Jiney J. Ryland, 2 Jan. 1805, Churchwell Curtis sec.
Butler, Major & Elizabeth Oliver, 29 Dec. 1790, John Farrar sec.

Byasea, John & Milley Russell, 21 Dec. 1807, Theophilus Russell sec.

Cabiness (Caviness) Charles & Lucy Worsham Ingram, 5 Jan. 1795,
        William Burton sec. Note from P. Ingram, father of Lucy
Cabiness, George & Jinny Elliott, 30 Nov. 1799, Thomas Finch sec.
        Note from Martin Elliott, father of Jinny

Callis, William & Frances Gregory, 13 Dec. 1790, Andrew Gregory sec.

Calloway, Achilles, of Pittsylvania Co. & Elizabeth Hudson, 9 Feb.
        1795, Richard Hudson sec.

Camp, George & Mary Palmer, 30 July 1772, Nicholas Maynard sec.
Camp, John & Mary Smith, 12 May 1783, George Tarry sec.
Camp, Richard, of Halifax Co. & Nancy Hudson, 11 Jan. 1802, William
    Hudson sec. Note from John Hudson, father of Nancy.

Campbell, Collin & Fanny Epperson, 30 Nov. 1785, John Campbell sec.

Cardin, Reuben & Stacy Bowen, 8 Jan. 1793, Zachariah Bowen sec. Note
    from John Cardin, father of Reuben - Note from James Boing.
Cardin, Robert & Lockey Hunt, 4 Jan. 1787, Joel Moore sec. Note from
    John Cardin, father of Robert, wit. Leonard Cardin & John
    Cardin. Note from William Hunt, father of Lockey, wit. Bery
    Hunt & Mary Bery.

Carter, Braxton & Polley Green, 9 June 1802, E. Green sec.
Carter, John & Polley Stevens, 12 Dec. 1788, Thomas Stevens sec.
Carter, Matthew & Sally Varnel, 13 Aug. 1804, William Bitchett sec.
Carter, Richard & Mary Haile, 14 Jan. 1793, Ellyson Crew, sec.
Carter, Robert & Jinney Naish, 18 Feb. 1802, Abel Naish sec.

Carleton, Gabriel & Elizabeth Edward, 14 Jan. 1788, John Edwards sec.

Carrel (Carrell-Carroll), James & Salley Greffies, 12 Dec. 1786, Mark
    Lambert Jackson sec.
Carrell, William & Mary Crowder, 3 Jan. 1788, Bailey Turner sec.

Carroll (Carrel-Carrell), Ezekiel & Martha Douglass, 13 Apr. 1805,
    Eli Elam sec.
Carroll, John & Amey Crowder, 28 Nov. 1793, Daniel Tucker sec.
Carroll, John & Anne Crowder, 23 Dec. 1793, Richard Fox sec.
Carroll, John & Caty Humphries Short, 22 Apr. 1797, Wm.Carroll sec.

Carrier, John & Elizabeth Parsons, 13 June 1785, Frans. Barnes sec.
    Note from Thomas Parsons, father of Elizabeth

Caviness (Cabiness), William & Elizabeth Culbreath, 8 Feb. 1796,
    Henry Hester & Thos. Culbreath sec.

Cazy, William & Polly Evans, 23 Dec. 1786, Kinchen Chavous sec.

Chavous, Allen & Salley Clanch, 7 Sept. 1804, Drury Johnson sec.
Chavous, Anthony & Rebecca Stewart, 10 Sept. 1792, Henry Royster sec.
Chavous, Boling & Suckey Thomason, 25 Jan. 1798, Banister Thomason
    sec. Note from Amy Thomason, mother of Suckey.
Chavous, Earby & Fanny McLin, 9 Mar. 1797, Thomas McLin sec.
Chavous, Jacob & Pheby Scott, 8 Dec. 1800, Thomas A. Jones & James
    Wilson sec. Note from James Mayne - wit. Champ Marable
Chavous, John & Sally Blair, 27 July 1801, Thomas Cypress sec.
Chavous, William & Pricilla Drew, 29 ____ 1806, Benj. Lewis &
    Richard Russell sec.
Chavous, Kitchen & Milley Chavous, 22 Dec.1788, Wm. Thomerson sec.
Chandler, Joel & Aryness Leigh, 12 Apr. 1774, Nathaniel Hix sec.
Chandler, Joel & Hannah Davis, 14 May 1807, David Chandler & Step
    P. Pool sec. Note from Step.P.Pool, G'dn. of Hannah

Chandler, Robert, of Granville, N. C. & Lucretia Graves, 11 Feb. 1797,
  John P. Finch sec. Note from Elijah & Lucretia Graves,
  parents of Lucretia.
Chandler, Samuel & Lina Stewart, 23 Dec. 1793, William Chandler sec.

Chambers, Nathaniel & Mary Small, 6 Sept. 1790, James Chambers sec.

Chambliss, James & Mary Stigall, 10 Nov. 1785, Mial Wall sec.

Cheatham, Daniel & Rebecca Cooper, 21 June 1790, William Drumright
  sec. Note from Elisha Arnold, G'dn. states that Rebecca
  is dau. of Francis Cooper - Wit. Bandy Walker & Jo.Burnett
Cheatham, James & Ann Wilson, 9 Feb. 1784, John Wilson sec.
Cheatham, James & Caty Johnson, 11 Jan. 1794, Wyatt Harper sec.
Cheatham, John & Nancy Vaughan, 23 Feb. 1808, Ambrose Vaughan sec.
Cheatham, Obadiah & Lucy Jones, 21 Dec. 1787, William Drumright sec.
  Note from Balaam Jones, father of Lucy.
Cheatham, Samuel & Elizabeth Keeton, 12 May 1800, Warner Keeton sec.
Cheatham, Samuel & Nancy Davis, 22 Dec. 1803, William Davis sec.

Christopher, Jacobus & Lurita Dennis _____ _____ Moses Overton sec.

Church, Robert & Elizth. Jones, 9 Dec. 1799, Richard Jones sec.

Cirkes, Jesse & Ellender Ornsby, 11 Nov. 1786, William Singleton sec.

Clay, Eleazar & Elizabeth Whitehead, 7 Jan. 1789, Richard White sec.
Clay, John & Salley Coleman, 11 Feb. 1805, James Coleman sec.
Clay, Tolbert & Nanney Harris, 7 Apr. 1805, John E. Harris sec.

Clark(Clarke), Archibald & Sarah Northington, 24 June 1807, Scar-
  borough Penticost sec. - Note from Nathan Northington,
  father of Sarah.
Clarke, Carter & Martha Farrar, 9 Nov. 1778, Edward Finch &
  Stephen Mabry sec. Note signed John & George Farrar.
Clark, Elisha & Nancy Waller, 2 Jan. 1810, John Waller sec.
Clark, Henry & Elizabeth Wilson, 6 Jan. 1801, Henry Wilson sec.
Clark, James & Nancy Williamson, 10 Dec. 1792, John Williamson sec.
Clark, Jesse & Martha Jones, 23 Oct. 1799, James Jones sec.
Clark, John S. & Ann E. Walker, 13 Sept. 1790, Henry Walker sec.
Clark, Joseph & Salley Mullins, 9 Feb. 1795, James Hudson sec.
Clarke, Joseph & Sarah Toone, 14 Dec. 1795, Bolling Clarke sec.
Clark, Richard & Caty Wall, 20 Jan. 1800, Richard Overbey sec.
Clark, William & Jinny Insco, 3 Sept. 1785, James Insco sec.
  Note from John Clark, father of William - wit. James
  Brown.

Claunch, Dennis & Nancy Beasley, 8 Nov. 1803, William Justice sec.
Claunch, Jeremiah & Prudence Jackson, 21 Mar. 1799, Sam'l.
  Allgood sec.
Claunch, Matthew & Elizabeth Allgood, 29 Aug. 1799, Sam'l.
  Allgood sec.
Claunch, William & Betsey Alvis, 5 Aug. 1793, William Blacketter
  sec. Note from Jeremiah Claunch, father of William -
  Note from David Alvis, father of Betsey.wit.Sherd Hicks

Clausel, Joseph B. & Susannah Brame, 23 Feb. 1799, John Puryear, Jr. sec.

Clausel, Wm. W. V. & Elizabeth Brame, 19 July, 1803, John Puryear sec.

Clardy, James & Luritta Daniel, 18 June, 1810, William Daniel sec.

Cleaton, Isham & Lucy Taylor, 8 Mar. 1809, William Cleaton sec.
Cleaton, John & Martha Taylor, 10 Nov. 1787, David Taylor sec.
Cleaton, Thomas & Nancy Webb, 27 Nov. 1787, Abel Dortch sec.
Cleaton, Thomas & Lucy Malone, 3 Mar. 1808, Thomas Nance sec.
Cleaton, Woodley & Salley Harris, 2 Jan. 1805, John Harris sec.

Clemmond, Matthew,& Elizabeth Allgood, 3 Mar. 1789, John Allgood sec.

Clements, Austis, of Charlotte Co. & Mary M. Mayne, 11 Feb. 1805, Henry W. Overbey sec. Note from James Mayne - wit. Thomas Westbrook.
Clements, Edmond & Sarah L. Weight, 12 Nov. 1805, Richard Moss sec.
Clements, William & Sarah Bignal, 5 June 1789, Joseph Speed sec.

Cliborne, Leo & Mary M. Stokes, 13 May 1799, John Powell, sec.

Cobbs, Thomas & Elizth. H. Phillips, 23 Oct. 1806, John Dortch sec.

Cocke, James & Elizabeth Moss, 26 July 1800, Lewis Moss sec.

Cole (Coles), Bartlett & Levina Tisdale, 27 Oct. 1789, Edward Tisdale sec.
Cole, James & Micah Beville, 13 Mar. 1797, Francis Neal sec.
Cole, Robert & Mary Stewart, 31 Dec. 1802, Martin Cousins sec.
Cole, Thomas & Anne Kirkland, 21 Dec. 1792, James Cole sec.

Coles (Cole) Tucker, of Albemarle Co. & Helen Skipwith, 21 May 1810, John S. Ravenscroft, of Lunenburg Co. sec. Note from Jean Skipwith, mother of Helen.

Coleman, Burwell & Martha Davis, 28 Jan. 1794, Isaac Davis sec. Note from James B. Davis, father of Martha - wit. Joel Davis
Coleman, Cain & Betsey Grigg, 11 Apr. 1794, Jesse Griggs sec. Note on bond: "This license was returned to me, with information that Cain Coleman was a married man, at the time he obtained it" Signed: W. Baskervill D. Ct. M.C.
Coleman, Cain & Sally Inge, 5 Jan. 1803, Rd. Taylor sec.
Coleman, Cain & Anne Reamy, 9 Jan. 1804, Richard Carter sec.
Coleman, Daniel of Pitsylvania Co. & Elizabeth Haskins, 14 Nov. 1791, H. Towns, of Halifax Co. sec. Note - Thomas Haskins father of Elizabeth
Coleman, Daniel & Susannah Overton, 14 Sept. 1801, John Overton sec.
Coleman, James & Sarah Whitehead, 14 Nov. 1785, Richard Swepson sec.

Coleman, John & Martha Pettus, 11 Dec. 1799, William Stone sec.
Coleman, Rederick & Lucy Daws, 18 Dec. 1794, Note: James Daws
Coleman, Thomas & Salley Rowlett, 5 Jan. 1799 - Note from William
    Rowlett, father of Salley.
Coleman, William B., of Spotsilvania Co. & Matilda Baptist, 2 June
    1803, Jos. N. Meredith sec. - Note from Wm. G. Baptist.

Coley, Davis & Elizabeth Matthews, 12 Mar. 1787, William Wells Green
    sec.
Coley, Isham & Frances Weakes, 9 Apr. 1787, George Tucker sec.
Coley, Thomas & Catherine Tucker, 24 Feb. 1800, Leonard Keeton sec.

Collier, Frederick & Ann Lark, 4 Sept. 1781, Edw. Pennington sec.
Collier, Howell & Hannah Creedle, 16 Nov. 1793, Lewis Collier sec.

Colley, Sam & Obedience Williams, 24 Mar. 1785, Thomas Clark sec.

Conner, William & Martha Carroll, 18 Sept. 1804, Dennis Roberts
    sec.

Connell, Benjamin & Martha Hatch, 27 Aug. 1788, William Taylor sec.
    Note from Freeman Hante, G'dn. & brother in law of Martha.
    wit. William Pennington & Julius Hite
Connell, James & Janney Pennington, 8 Aug. 1785, John Adams sec.

Connaway, John & Susanna Royster, 19 Nov. 1819, Alexander B. Pur-
    year sec.

Cook, Hurbert & Penelope Taylor, 20 Dec. 1802, John Taylor sec.
Cook, Herbert & Salley Walker, 6 Nov. 1805, Tilman Elder sec.
Cook, Kirby & Lizey Adams, 2 Jan. 1788, Thomas Adams sec.
Cook, William & Fanney Rainey, 5 May 1803, Buchner Raney sec.

Cooper, Francis & Betty Arnold, 25 Apr. 1769, James Arnold sec.

Couch, John & Susanna Smith, 25 Oct. 1799, Archer Smith sec.
Couch, Thomas & Sarah Gregory, 26 Nov. 1801, Archibald Smith sec.

Couzens (Cousins) Peter & Phibby A. Marshall, 15 Dec. 1800,
    Francis Marshall sec.

Cousins (Couzens), Austin & Elizabeth Brandon _____ 18__, Robert
    Cole sec.
Cousins, Martin & Jincey Cole, 31 Dec. 1802, Robert Cole sec.

Cox, Archer & Polley Lewis Hatsel, 8 Feb. 1802, John Talley sec.
Cox, Bannister & Rebecca Barnes, 26 Oct. 1803, John Pritchett sec.
Cox, Bartley & Susanna Carleton, 12 Nov. 1781, Asa Oliver sec.
Cox, Bartley & Lucy Allgood, 18 Sept. 1786, Allen Burton sec.
Cox, Edward & Dianna Holloway, 31 Dec. 1767, Henry Delony sec.
Cox, Edward & Salley Brown, 3 Jan. 1795, Joseph Hamilton sec.
Cox, John, Jr. & Martha B. Hall, 11 July 1803, Wm. Marshall sec.
Cox, Kennon & Pricilla Smith, 4 Mar. 1803, John Morgan sec.
Cox, Samuel & Salley Hutt, 16 July 1806, Archer Cox sec.

Cox, Thomas & Margary Hudson, 17 Mar. 1794, David Hudson sec.
Cox, Thomas & Mary Draper, 7 Mar. 1796, Thomas Pritchett sec.

Craig, Rev. James, of Lunenburg Co. & Mary Tarry, Spinster, 19 Feb.
1766, Edmond Taylor sec.

Craddock, David & Nancy Neal, 25 Oct. 1800, G. H. Baskervill sec.

Crew, Ellyson & Salley Carter, 4 June 1790, Winkfield Hayes sec.
Crew, Charles & Nancy Hut, 11 Jan. 1808, Samuel Cox sec.
Crews, John & Sarah Nash, 25 July 1782, Nath. Moss sec.

Crenshaw, John & Elizabeth Walker, 26 Dec. 1801, Thomas A.Jones sec.

Creath, William & Lucy Brame, 11 June 1792, H. C. Speed sec. George
Craighead & Reuben Vaughan sec. Note from Elizabeth Brame,
mother of Elizabeth.

Creedle, Drury & Patsy Mason, 22 Sept. 1798, Jeremiah Adams sec.
Creedle, Edmond & Mary Anne Talley, 11 Feb.1791,Drury Creedle sec.
Crowder, Abraham & Martha Loyd, 30 Dec. 1805, Elijah Crowder sec.
Crowder, Anderson & Polley Brummell, 20 Jan. 1796, Abram Crowder sec.
Crowder, David & Easter Jones, 30 Apr. 1795, Charles Kelley Jones
sec.
Crowder, Elijah & Rebekah Loyd, 9 Aug. 1803, Richard Crowder sec.
Crowder, Fred K. & Milley Bowers, 4 Dec. 1797, James Bowen sec.
Crowder, Gardiner & Amy Tucker, 4 Dec. 1788, David Crowder sec.
Crowder, George & Nancy Bailey, 26 Jan. 1798, Richard Crowder sec.
Crowder, George, & Sally Wright, 28 Oct. 1803, Elijah Crowder sec.
Crowder, James & Patsy Minor, 28 Dec. 1795, George Minor sec.
Crowder, James & Elizabeth Tucker, 12 Dec. 1810, Daniel Tucker sec.
Crowder, Larkin & Lucy Rottenberry, 29 Sept. 1789, Sam'l Rotten-
berry sec.
Crowder, Miles T. & Susannah B. Jeffries, 27 Oct. 1806, Achilles
Jeffries sec.
Crowder, Nathaniel & Martha Rainey, 25 Nov. 1805, Buckner Rainey
sec.
Crowder, Richard & Lucey Clausel, 13 Feb. 1797, Richard Hutcheson
sec.
Crowder, Robert & Lively Hester, 2 Sept. 1788, Absolom Hester sec.
Crowder, Thomas & Fanney Rhodes, 29 Mar. 1785, John Rhodes sec.
Crowder, Thomas & Elizabeth Puryear, 14 Feb. 1786, Solomon Draper
sec.
Crowder, Thomas & Patsy Russell, 18 Dec. 1787, Thomas Jones sec.
Note from Ann Russell, mother of Patsy - wit. Josiah & Mary
Daly.

Crow, John & Martha Easter, 28 Dec. 1802, Jeremiah Adams sec.
Crow, William & Nancy Thompson, 3 Dec. 1799, Charles Thompson sec.
Note from John Crow, father of William.

Crook, William & Martha Edwards, 11 Apr. 1791, John Edwards, Jr.sec.

Crutchfield, Adams & Nancy House, 3 Jan. 1810, Bartley Cheatham sec.

Crutchfield, Samuel & Patsey Ellis, 25 Dec. 1804, Jesse Perkinson sec.

Culbreath, James & Polley Monroe, 12 Dec. 1803, Ellyson Crew sec.
Culbreath, John & Mary Clark, 13 Dec. 1790, Elijah Graves sec.
Culbreath, Thomas & Polley Culbreath, 8 May 1809, Hughes Matthews sec.
Culbreath, William & Temple Wiles, 13 Mar. 1804, Isaac Pinson sec.

Cullthorp, John & Mary Crowder, 10 Feb. 1784, Samuel Edmondson sec.

Cunningham, James & Alice Marshall, 10 July 1809, Robert Marshall sec.
Cunningham, William & Salley Marshall, 10 Dec. 1798, Robert Marshall
    sec.

Curtis, Churchwell & Rebecca Johnson, 17 June 1801, Jesse Curtis sec.
Curtis, Elie & Nancy Drummond, 28 Jan. 1794, William Baskervill &
    Thomas Drummond sec.
Curtis, Elemeleck & Polley Nunnelly, 2 Jan. 1798, Micajah Gwartney
    sec.
Curtis, Jesse & Mary Moore, 27 Feb. 1792, James Moore sec.
Curtis, John & Betsey Johnson, 19 Dec. 1804, Crafford McDaniel, sec.
Curtis, Zachariah & Salley Powers, 16 Feb. 1795, Dury Creedle sec.

Cuts, William & Mary Mullins, 22 Nov. 1791, John Ragsdale sec.

Dacus, Alexander, of Lunenburg Co. & Jane Duprey, 17 Nov. 1789,
    Drury Duprey sec/

Daley (Daly), Ambrose & Sarah Taylor, 30 Jan. 1809, James Taylor
    sec.
Daly Daniel & Elizabeth Holmes, 22 Dec. 1788, Sherwood Smith sec.
Daley, Daniel & Elizabeth Bugg, 1 July 1794, Abel Dortch sec.
Daly, John & Mary Russell, 11 Mar. 1782, Sam'l. Goode sec.
Daly, Josiah & Jinney McKinney, 21 Oct. 1795, Bennett Goodman sec.
Daly, Josiah, Jr. & Mary Moody, 14 Nov. 1800, John Daly, Jr. sec.
Daley, Vines & Rebecca Adams, 14 Oct. 1795, William Adams sec.
Daly, William & Lucy Abernathy, 10 Mar. 1807, Tignal Abernathy,Jr.
    sec. Note from Burwell Abernathy, father of Lucy.

Dance, Stephen & Elizabeth Briggs, 11 May 1805, Charles Ogburn
    sec.

Daniel, Martin & Polly Daniel, 9 June 1800, Thomas Daniel sec.
Daniel, Samuel & Martha Short, 13 Nov. 1809, Henry Wall sec.
Daniel, Starky & Frances Royster, 4 Jan. 1803, Robert Shanks sec.
Daniel, Walter & Jean Puryear, 2 May, 1804, Benjamin Bugg sec.
    Note from Peter Bailey - wit. Thomas Allen & John White.
Daniel, William & Elizabeth Wootton, 9 Jan. 1806, John Winckler
    sec.
Daniel, William & Elizabeth Short, 29 June 1807, Wyatt short sec.

Davis, Charles & Elizabeth Hopkins, 11 Dec. 1784, John Hopkins
    sec.

Davis, Hardaway, & Elizabeth Davis, 12 Aug. 1771, Capt. William Davis
    sec. Note from Hardaway Davis.
Davis, James & Sarah Holmes, 9 Mar. 1767, John Ballard, Jr. sec.
Davis, John & Rebecca Watson, 11 Nov. 1778, Michael Watson sec.
Davis, John, Jr. & Susanna Swepson, 28 Mar. 1786, Richard Swepson sec.
Davis, John & Phebey Floyd, 12 Nov. 1787, Charles Floyd sec.
Davis, John, Jr. & Rebecca Ballard, 10 Dec. 1804, John Holmes, Jr.
    sec.
Davis, Joshua & Nancy Wright, 3 Jan. 1805, William Wright sec.
Davis, Matthew H. & Polley Lett, 22 Dec. 1801, Hardaway Lett sec.
    Note from Joseph Lett, Sr., father of Polley.
Davis, William, of Brunswick Co. & Martha Thompson, 17 Sept. 1765,
    Wells Thompson sec.
Davis, William & Mary Cheatham, 10 Oct. 1804, Daniel Cheatham sec.

Daws, James & Elizabeth L. Ferrell, 12 June, 1798, Hubbard Ferrell
    sec.

Decker, Henry & Patsey Talley, 30 Dec. 1791, Hansel Talley & Wm.
    Decker sec.

Dedman, Henry & Jincy White, 11 May 1795, William White sec.
Dedman, John & Elizabeth White, 11 Feb. 1799, Henry H. Dedman sec.

DeGraffenried, Francis & Ermin Boswell, 12 Nov. 1781, Asa Oliver
    sec. Note from Joseph Boswell.

Delony, Edward & Elizabeth Lucas, 25 Nov. 1796, Wm. Delony sec.
    Note from William Lucas, father of Elizabeth

Dennis, Matthew & Nancy Griffin, 8 May, 1797, Jacobus Christopher,
    sec.

Dickens, Samuel & Jane Vaughan, 22 May 1801, John Wilson sec.

Dixon, Benjamin & Elzth. Wagstaff, 20 Nov. 1800, John Wagstaff
    sec.

Douglass, David & Martha Jones, 6 Nov. 1777, Francis Lightfoot
    sec.
Douglas, James & Nancy Johnson, 21 Oct. 1808, Terasha Johnson sec.

"Dortch" page 16.

Drumright, Ephriam & Elizabeth Pennington, 3 ___ 1808.
Drumright, James & Lytha Crowder, 9 Oct. 1794, William Drumright
    sec. Note from Richard Crowder, father of Lytha - wit.
    Josiah Floyd & Thomas Andrews.
Drumright, Thomas & Sarah Osling Williams, 18 Jan. 1804, Lewis
    Williams sec.
Drumright, William, Jr. & Libelar Crowder, 14 July, 1797, Wm.
    Drumright & Richard Crowder sec.
Drumright, William, Jr. & Lucy Gee, 28 Feb. 1803, Thomas Drum-
    right sec. Note from Jones Gee, father of Lucy - wit.
    William Drumright, Sr. & Benj. Gee.

Drummond, David & Nancy Johnson, 27 Nov. 1787, Howell Johnson sec.
Note from James Johnson.

Dugger, William, of Brunswick Co. & Jean Stainback, 23 Oct. 1804,
James Stainback sec.

Dunnington, Reuben & Polly Wright, 11 July 1798, William Wright sec.

Dunston, Miles & Nancy Stewart, 18 Feb. 1802, Thomas Spence sec.

Duprey (Dupree), Drury & Ann Atkinson, 8 Mar. 1784, John Crews sec.
Note from Median Atkinson, parent of Ann - Note from
Lewis Dupree, father of Drury.
Dupree, John, of Brunswick Co. & Nancy Short, 11 Dec. 1787, Thomas
Buford sec. Note from Jacob & Mary Short.
Duprey, Lewis & Median edian Atkinson, 11 Oct. 1784, Drury Duprey
sec.

Duty, Benj. & Mary Wagstaff, 20 Nov. 1809, Raggel Wagstaff sec.
Note from John Wagstaff, father of Mary.

Dortch, Abel & Salley Taylor, 24 May 1785, Goodwyn Taylor sec.
Dortch, Abel & Mary Holmes, 29 Oct. 1793, David Dortch sec.
Dortch, David & Betsey Taylor, 30 May 1798, Abel Dortch sec.
Dortch, Jesse & Ora Saunders, 24 Jan. 1792, Jacob Bugg sec.
Note from Mary Saunders, mother of Ora - wit. Edmond
Bugg
Dortch, Lewis & Mary Speed, 2 Jan. 1796, James Speed sec.
Dortch, Newman & Sarah Speed, 29 Mar. 1800, John Dortch sec.
Dortch, Noah & Ann Lucas, 25 Apr. 1780, W. Baskervill sec.
Dortch, William & Susanna Burton, 29 Sept. 1786, Robert Penning-
ton sec.

Earles, Presley & Elizabeth Pointer, 13 May 1807, Robert Nanny
sec.

Edards, Thomas & Caty Wall, 10 Mar. 1800, Thomas Daniel sec.

Edmunds, Abel & Dolley Hudgins, 24 Feb. 1800, James Hudgins sec.

Edmonson (Edmondson-Edmundson), Banister & Janey Davis, 16 Dec.
1793, George B. Hamner, sec. Note from John Davis
father of Janey
Edmundson, Benjamin & Keziah Hood, 17 Oct. 1785, Charles Hood sec.
Edmondson, John & Judith Clay, 6 Oct. 1792, Coleman Edmondson sec.
Edmondson, Robert Spilsbury & Nancy Singleton, 29 Jan. 1803,
Thomas Crowder sec. Note from Patsey Singleton, mother
of Nancy.
Edmondson, Thomas & Milley Arnold, 8 Aug. 1796, Jere Arnold sec.

Edwards, George R. & Catherine Simmons, 12 Jan. 1797, Joseph
Simmons sec.
Edwards, John & Sarah Hyde, 8 Nov. 1784, Burell Russell sec.

Edwards, Thomas & Agnes Hobson, 6 Nov. 1798, Charles Patterson sec.
Edwards, William & Sarah Kirkland, 13 Feb. 1798, Jeffrey Mustian sec.

Elam (Eloam), Alexander & Janey Norment, 14 Nov. 1785, Thos. Norment
    sec.
Elam, Edward & Martha Smith, 13 Nov. 1786, Edward Finch sec. Note
    from John Smith, father of Martha.
Elam, John & Polley W. Garner, 23 Oct. 1797, Archibald Clark sec.
    Note from James Garner, father of Polley.
Elam, John & Elizabeth Elam, 13 Oct. 1806, James Hunt sec.
Eloam, Peter & Susanna Gregory, 8 Aug. 1795, Andrew Gregory sec.
Elam, Samuel & Martha Garner, 13 Oct. 1800, John Elam sec. Note
    from James Garner, father of Martha.
Elam, William & Patience Hurt, 19 Nov. 1810, William Hurt sec.

Elder, Tilman & Elizabeth Walker, 17 Dec. 1798, John Holloway sec.

Elibeck, John D. & Elizabeth Hutcheson, 18 July 1808, John Hutche-
    son (S.C.) sec.

Ellington, David & Letilia Cox, 2 Dec. 1793, Thomas Greer sec.
Ellington, William & Leannah Johnson, 17 Dec. 1807, John Johnson
    sec.

Elliott, William & Rebecca Boothe, 20 Dec. 1809, Reuben Boothe sec.

Epperson, Joseph & Polley Hunley, 10 Oct. 1803, William Hunley sec.

Eubank, James & Susanna Dailey, 1 Dec. 1801, John Furguson sec.
Eubank, William & Mary A. Holmes, 15 Jan. 1810, Pennington Holmes
    sec.

Evans, Charles & Martha Jeffries, 17 Aug. 1796, Kenchin Chavous sec.
Evans, Evan & Polly Lunsford, 24 Dec. 1807, John Wright sec.
Evans, Isaac & Dicy Stewart, 24 Dec. 1792, W. Baskervill sec.
Evans, John & Temperance Clay, 5 Nov. 1792, John F. Reazon sec.
Evans, John & Patsey Massey, 11 Sept. 1800, Stephen Evans sec.
Evans, Ludwell & Mary Hogan, 25 Feb. 1783, Edward Finch sec. Note
    from Edward Hogan, father of Mary.
Evans, Ludwell & Jane D. Hardy, 19 Nov. 1810, John S. Jeffries sec.
Evans, Matthew & Beckey Barnett, 5 Oct. 1804, John Barnett sec.
Evans, Peter & Elizabeth Overby, 1 Sept. 1792, Jeremiah Singleton
    sec. Note from Tary Overby, father of Elizabeth
Evans, Robin & Amy Stewart, 13 Feb. 1809, James Chavous sec.
Evans, Starling & Letty Thompson, 12 Oct. 180_, Bernard Thompson sec.
Evans, Stephen & Milley Mason, 22 Nov. 1797, Araninas Grainger sec.
Evans, William & Ede Hogan, 10 Apr. 1775, Edward Morgan sec.
Eveans, William & Polley Walker, 8 Dec. 1802, Wilson Walker sec.

Ezell, Balaam & Elizabeth Mayo, 27 Dec. 1803, Thomas Owen sec.
Ezell, Balaam, Jr. & Sally Childers, 14 Nov. 1808, Balaam Ezell,Sr.
    sec.
Ezell, Berryman & Phebe Hamblin, 8 Aug. 1803, Peter Hamblin sec.
    Note from Thomas Hamblin, father of Phebe.

Farmer, Thomas & Susa Stone, 9 Dec. 1804, Jordan Stone sec.

Fargeson, Joseph & Elizabeth Holloway, 6 Feb. 1789, Ben Ferrell sec.
Fargeson, Peter T. & Elizabeth Jackson, 5 July 1809, Cavil Jackson sec.

Farley, James, of Amelia Co. & Martha Evans, 26 July 1786, Henry
  Farley sec. Note from James Farley, father of James - Note
  from Stephen Evans, father of Martha.

Farrar, Abel & Sarah Clark, 11 Aug. 1788, Matthew Langaster Easter
  sec.
Farrar, George & Elizabeth Boyd, 22 Aug. 1783, Richard Swepson, Jr.
  sec.
Farrar, John & Ann Baskervill, 24 Dec. 1794, Robert Baskervill sec.
Farrar, John & Nancy Hunt, 13 June 1808, John P. Finch sec.
Farrar, Richardson & Susanna Baskervill, 12 June, 1810, Newman Dortch
  sec.
Farrar, Samuel & Elizabeth Phillips, 10 Nov. 1786, Hardy Jones sec.
Farrar, Thomas & Sarah Farrar, 15 Dec. 1790, James Faucet sec.
Farrar, William & Lucy Medley, 24 July 1780, John Farrar sec.

Faulkner, Johnson & Mary Griffin, 8 Apr. 1799, Stephen P. Pool sec.
  Note from William Griffin, father of Mary.

Feagins, John & Patty Lanier, 5 Jan. 1786, John Saunders sec.
Feagin, Richardson & Martha Apperson, dau. David Apperson, 3 Feb.
  1779, Thomas Pynsent sec.

Feild, Edmond & Mary Tanner, 14 Sept. 1807, G. H. Baskervill sec.
Feild, James & Henryetta Marine, 17 Feb. 1789, Thomas Anderson sec.
Feild, John S. & Jean Walker, 9 June 1788, Henry Walker sec.
Feild, Thomas & Mary White, 11 Jan. 1782, James Anderson sec.

Ferrell, Benjamin & Mary Burton, 12 Mar. 1770, James Ferrell sec.
Ferrell, Ben. & Sarah Collier, 13 Dec. 1773, Howell Collier sec.
Ferrell, Ben & Ann Dortch, 11 Feb. 1784, W. Baskervill sec.

Finch, Edw. & Jane Puryear, 13 Mar. 1775, John Puryear sec.
Finch, George & Janey Short, 7 Dec. 1796, Freeman Short sec.
Finch, George & Amy Arnold, 22 Sept. 1803, Jeremiah Arnold sec.
Finch, Henry & Martha Steagall, 2 June, 1794, Robert Pennington sec.
Finch, John & Elizabeth Farrar, 18 Apr. 1787, Peter Farrar sec.
  Note from John Farrar, father of Elizabeth - wit. Charly
  Farrar & H. G. Carleton.
Finch, John P. & Nancy Graves, 14 Sept. 1795, Elijah Graves sec.
Finch, William & Rebecca Clay, 14 Aug. 1775, Edward Finch sec.
  Note from Henry Clay - wit. John Clay & John Bruce.
Finch, William & Elizabeth Christopher, 31 Jan. 1780, William
  Christopher sec.

Fisher, Jonathan & Susannah Booth, 5 May 1801, Reuben Booth sec.

Floyd, Drury & Betsey Lanier, 25 Oct. 1791, Josiah Floyd sec.
  Note from Samuel Lanier, father of Betsey - wit. Morris
  Floyd, Allan Lanier & Davy Ezell.

19

Floyd, Josiah & Rebecca Bugg, 28 Mar. 1810, Jesse Bugg sec.

Flood, William & Moly Harris Brogdon, 12 Nov. 1785, Thomas Macklin sec.
Note from William Brogdon.

Flynne, John & Salley Green, 11 Apr. 1791, David Green sec.

Fountaine, Joseph & Mary Goode, 8 Feb. 1773, Edward Goode sec.

Fowler, Starling & Sarah Ellis, 4 Dec. 1802, Jesse Perkinson sec.

Fox, Benjamin & Martha Norvell, 9 May 1792, Young Norvell sec.
Fox, Richard & Mary Rainey, 22 Mar. 1775, William Davis sec.
Fox, Richard & Nancy Wright, 4 Oct. 1792, Solomon Pittillo sec.
Fox, Robert & Polley Warren, 26 Nov. 1801, John Warren sec.

Fraser (Frasar-Frazer), Daniel & Martha Fargeson, 14 Feb. 1805,
John Fraser sec.
Frazer, James, of Orange Co., N. C. & Hoppy Brame, dau. R. Brame,
3 June, 1778, John Brame sec.
Frasar, John, of Prince Edward Co. & Lucy Adams, 4 Jan. 1780,
William Crutchfield sec.

Francis, John & Elizabeth Epperson, 8 Sept. 1794, Joseph Townes sec.

Freeman, Benjamin & Mary Roberts, 26 May 1803, Stephen Roberts sec.
Freeman, Gidian & Mary Elam, 10 Jan. 1803, Philiman Hurt sec.
Freeman, John & Lucy Hudson, 9 Oct. 1798, Stephen Hudson sec. Note
from George Freeman, father of John.
Freeman, John & Agga Walker, 22 July 1806, John Johnson sec.

Gabard, John & Betsey Curtis, 25 Feb. 1792, Ely Curton sec.

Garner, James & Lucy Eodins, 11 Jan. 1790, Thos. Dance sec.
Garner, James & Mary Smith, 10 Nov. 1806, Hume R. Feild sec.
Garner, Vinson & Nancy Jeffries, 9 Nov. 1807, Richard Jeffries sec.

Garland, Capt. Thomas, of Lunenburg Co. & Polley Lowry, 8 July
1783, John Speed sec. Note from John Radsdale, G'dn. of
Polley.

Garrall, William & Mary Roberts, 9 Nov. 1795, Thomas Massey sec.

Gayle, John, of Halifax Co. & Nancy Whitehead, 23 Mar. 1793,
William Whitehead sec. Note from Jos. Coleman.

Gee, James, of Lunenburg Co. & Lucy Bugg, 6 Feb. 1797, John Bugg
sec. Note from Neavil Gee, father of James, wit.
Jones & Mary Gee.
Gee, James Street & Nancy Gee, 10 Nov. 1798, Jones Gee sec.
Gee, Jeremiah & Patsey Andrews, 19 Nov. 1804, Varney Andrews sec.
Gee, Neavil & Elizabeth Andrews, 19 July, 1797, Varn Andrew sec.
Notes from Neavil Gee, father of Neavil & George And-
rews, father of Elizabeth

Gee, Peter R. & Elizabeth H. Daly, 18 Jan. 1808, Tignal Abernathy sec.
Gee, William, of Lunenburg Co. & Caty Jones, 12 Dec. 1787, Vermy
Andrews sec.

George, Jeremiah & Mary Lambert, 6 June 1797, Thomas Lambert sec.

Giles, Edward & Martha Ezell, 31 Jan. 1807, Thomas Nance sec.
Giles, William & Lucy Standley, 17 Dec. 1804, James Standley sec.
Gill, William & Judith Maynard, 8 Dec. 1783, Nicholas Maynard sec.

Gillispie, Martin & Elizabeth Elam, 10 Feb. 1806, H. H. Dedmon sec.

Glasgow, Richard & Amey Chappell, 20 Dec. 1785, Philip Reckes sec.

Glidenwell, John & Anne Whitlow, 20 Aug. 1785, Thomas Whitlow sec.

Gloves, Daniel & Mary Westmoreland, 8 Nov. 1806, Robert Westmoreland sec.

Goen, Frederick & Suckee Chavous, 9 Mar. 1789, Frederick Ivey sec.
Note from Henry Chavous, Sr. - wit. James Stewart, Robert
Singleton & Belar Chavous.

Goode, Edward & Joice Holmes, 13 Dec. 1798, Richard Cox sec.
Goode, John & Martha Moore, 19 Apr. 1790, John Wilson, Jr. sec.
Goode, John B. & Permelia B. Hendrick, 2 July, 1804, Amasa Palmer
sec.
Goode, John & Mary Jones, 8 May 1809, William G. Goode sec. Note
from Edward Jones, father of Mary.
Goode, Joseph & Martha Birchett, 31 Aug. 1790, Philip Morgan sec.
Goode, Richard & Nancy Charlotte Poindexter, 8 Oct. 1781, Phil
Poindexter sec.
Goode, Samuel & Mary Armistead Burwell, 28 Sept. 1786, Nicholas
Bilbo sec.   Note from Lewis Burwell, father of Mary
Goode, William G. & Mary Tabb, 2 Sept. 1798, G. H. Baskervill sec.

Goodwin, Beal & Elizabeth Frazer, 10 Dec. 1798, James Brame sec.
Note from H. Frazer, father of Elizabeth.
Goodwin, Samuel, of Botetourt & Lucy Smith, 22 Mar. 1793, Thomas
Hord sec. Note from Mary Hord, mother of Lucy.

Gooch, Joseph, of Granville Co., N. C. & Anne Lockett, 27 June
1794.

Graves, Frederick & Nancy Brandon, 20 Dec. 1800, Ephriam Drew
sec.
Graves, Howel & Elizabeth Hunt, 13 Apr. 1801, James Hunt sec.
Graves, Ralph & Elizabeth Graves, 9 Feb. 1789, Henry Walker sec.
Graves, Thomas & Mary Harris, 26 Dec. 1808, John Stembridge sec.
Graves, William & Frances Elam, 14 Oct. 1795, Thomas Graves sec.

Gresham, Gregory & Susannah Smith, 23 July 1806, Thomas Smith sec.
Note from Asa Gresham - wit. Gregory B. Hudson & Thomas
Smith. Note from William Smith, father of Susannah.

Gregory, Bannister & Susanna Griffin, 29 Aug. 1808, Elijah Griffin sec.
Gregory, Elijah & Nancy Moody, 8 June, 1801, Robert Smith sec.
Gregory, James & Sarah Doggett, 14 Sept. 1801, John Levansbow sec.
Gregory, John & Polley Apperson, 19 Dec. 1786, John Apperson, Sr. sec.
    Note from David Apperson, father of Polley, wit. John
    Apperson & Richard Jones.
Gregory, Nathaniel & Mary Anne Beckley, ___ Jan. 1787, Edw. L. Tabb sec.
Gregory, Roger & Elizabeth Bugg (note signed Speed) 21 Oct. 1791,
    Sherwood Bugg sec.

Green, Archibald & Judith Taylor, 11 Oct. 1802, Thomas Rowlet sec.
Green, James & Nancy Yancey, 9 Jan. 1792, William Hendrick sec.
Green, Lewis & Elizabeth Crawley, 8 Sept. 1788, John Baskervill sec.
Green, Thomas, of Lunenburg Co. & Francinac Cox, 22 Mar. 1792, John
    Cox sec.
Green, William W. & Mary Poindexter, 3 Jan. 1803, G. H. Baskervill
    sec.

Greenwood, James & Jane Sanders, 10 May 1779, James Hall sec.
Greenwood, James & Henrietta Hester, 9 June 1794, Henry H. Dedmon
    sec.
Greenwood, Thomas, Jr. & Martha Williams, 8 Oct. 1792, James T.
    Hayes sec. Note from James Hester, father of Martha.

Grigg, Burwell & Lobia Elam, 8 Oct. 1787, Alex. Elam sec.
Grigg, Drury & Anna Chavous, 13 Apr. 1807, Saunders Harris sec.
Grigg, James & Martha Elam, 11 Dec. 1786, James Elam sec.
Grigg, Lewis & Patsey Malone, 30 Mar. 1808, Thomas Cleaton sec.
Grigg, Randolph & Elizabeth Jordan, 17 Dec. 1805, Samuel Jordan
    sec. Note from Mary Jordan, mother of Elizabeth
Grigg, William & Mary W. Jordan, 8 Dec. 1800, John Matthews sec.

Griffith, John & Rainey Rottenberry, 14 Dec. 1790, John Lambert
    sec. Note from John Griffith, father of John - wit. Thomas
    Griffith.

Griffin, James & Polley Tindal, 14 Dec. 1807, Overton Wiles sec.
Griffin, John & Elizabeth Yancey, 11 Aug. 1794, Robert Williamson
    sec.
Griffin, William & Edna Blanks, 26 Sept. 1805, Jos. Blanks sec.

Grymes, Benjamin & Ann Nicholas, Spinster, 22 Dec. 1778, John
    Nicholas sec.

Guy, Daniel & Nancy Erls, 26 Feb. 1806, William Chandler sec.

Gwartney, John & Willey Underwood, 4 Dec. 1806, William Gwartney
    sec.
Gwartney, William & Agnes Colley, 23 May 1801, James Brown sec.

Halecomb, Philamon, of Prince Edward Co. & Lucy Anderson, 13 Dec.
    1784, Charles Lewis sec.

Haile, Dudley & Mary Willis, 10 Dec. 1781, Thomas Haile sec.
Haile, Dudley & Susanna Smith, 10 Feb. 1794, Harrison Winn sec.
Haile, Dudley & Patsey Carter, 12 Jan. 1795, William Willis sec.
Haile, Lemon & Eliza Avory, 19 June 1802, Elijah Avery sec.
Haile, Thomas & Sally Rudd, 17 Dec. 1804, Harwood Rudd sec.
Haile, Thomas & Nancy Blacketter, 25 Sept. 1805, Harwood Rudd sec.

Hailey (Haley), David & Lucy Crow, 3 Dec. 1804, Jacksonias Towler sec.

Haley (Hailey), David & Elizabeth Brooks, 8 Dec. 1783, Elijah Graves
     sec.
Haley, John & Dycy Blanks, 8 July, 1799, Elijah Griffin sec. Note
     from Joseph Blanks, father of Dycy.
Haley, Richard & Nancy Wilson, 26 Jan. 1805, John E. Harris sec.
Haley, Thomas & Elizabeth Gold, 9 June 1784, Dan Colde sec.

Hall, Miles & Susanna Marshall, 4 May 1781, Richard Winn sec. Note
     from James Hall, father of Miles - wit. William Finch &
     Abner Locket - Note from Daney Maccraw, G'dn. of Susanna.
Hall, Miles & Nancey Cox, 8 Sept. 1806, John Cox sec.
Hall, Richard Carter & Elizabeth Mayes, 11 Aug. 1794, John Hall
     sec. Note from John Mayes, father of Elizabeth.
Hall, William & Elizabeth Bradley, 6 Dec. 1802, John Bradley sec.
Hall, Zachariah & Sophia Malone, 4 Dec. 1792, Thomas Roberts sec.

Hamlin (Hamblin), William B. & Christian Burwell, 18 Dec. 1794,
     Daniel Mayo sec. Notes from Mary Hamlin, mother of
     William & Lewis Burwell, father of Christian.

Hamblin (Hamlin) John & Milley Daniel, 13 July 1807, Stephen Stone
     sec. Note from Marten Daniel, father of Milley.
Hamblin, Thomas & Jean Childress, 10 Nov. 1806, Balaam Ezell sec.

Hammond, Frederick & Polley Stewart, 14 Aug. 1807, Frederick Dyson
     sec.

Hamner, George B. & Anne Edmundson, 16 Dec. 1793, Banister Edmon-
     son sec.
Hamner, John & Molley Whobery, 22 Dec. 1790, John Whobery sec.

Hamlett, William, of Halifax & Mary Brooke, 27 Oct. 1789, Gabe
     Carleton sec.

Hamilton, Andrew, of Prince George Co. & Elizabeth Skinner, 14
     Feb. 1782, Josiah Daly sec.
Hamilton, Baxter & Prissey Bailey, 10 Jan. 1798, Robert Roberts
     sec.
Hamilton, John & Polley Hatsel, 12 Jan. 1795, Stephen Hatsel sec.
Hamilton, Joseph & Sarah Cox, 16 May 1791, Edward Hatsel sec.
     Note from Thomas Burnett.
Hamilton, Walter & Elizabeth Hatsel, 24 Aug, 1785, Mary Hatsel sec.
Hamilton, William & Nancey Christopher, 14 Jan. 1799, William
     Christopher sec.

Hanvell, Samuel & Martha Hanvell, 18 Dec. 1804, William Hanvell sec.
Note from James Hanvall.

Hansard, Richard & Sarah Speed, 12 Dec. 1774, Robert Ballard sec.
Hanserd, Richard & Sarah Ferguson, 18 June 1801, John Dortch sec.

Harper, John & Martha Pennington, 7 Dec. 1785, John Pennington sec.
Note from John Harper, father of John.
Harper, Thomas, of Dinwiddie Co. & Lucy Gilham Booth, 22 Jan. 1791,
Thomas Booth sec.
Harper, Wyatt & Mary M. Pennington, 29 July 1799, William Pennington
sec.

Hargrove, Bennitt & Biddy Lambert, 23 Jan. 1788, Matthew Smith sec.
Hargrove, James & Nancy Thomas, 14 Dec. 1797, John Thomas sec.

Hardy, James & Mary Wilson, 12 Jan. 1801, John Boswell sec.

Harrison, Greenwood & Susannah Mullins, 11 Feb. 1799, Edward Hollo-
way sec.
Harrison, James & Tabitha Webb, 5 Dec. 1801, Abdias P. Webb sec.
Note from E. Webb.
Harrison, John, of North Hampton Co. N. C. & Lelilah Parham, 22
Mar. 1792, William Kirks, of Orange, N. C., sec.
Harrison, Robert & Martha Baugh, 11 Jan. 1787, William Baugh sec.
Harrison, William & Margaret Wade, 16 Nov. 1790, Absolom Husting
sec.

Harris, Allin & Susanna Harris, 1 Mar. 1800, James Reamy sec.
Note from Reuben Harris, father of Susanna.
Harris, Drury & Patsey Butler, 10 Oct. 1803, Charles Carter sec.
Note from John Butler, father of Patsey.
Harris, Henry & Polly Roper, 20 Oct. 1809, Wilson Harris sec.
Harris, Ivey & Judith Algood, __ Dec. 1809, John Algood sec.
Harris, James & Rebecca Nolley, 20 Dec. 1806, Nevison Nolley sec.
Harris, Jeremiah & Lydia Chavous, 13 Nov. 1797, James Chavis sec.
Harris, John & Sarah Berry, 25 Dec. 1786, George Hudson sec.
Harris, John & Rittah Stewart, 27 Dec, 1802, Jere Harris sec.
Harris, John & Martha Crutchfield, 19 Dec. 1803, William Crutch-
field sec.
Harris, Martin, & Patsey Reamey, 14 Dec. 1807, William Harris sec.
Harris, Reuben & Sarah Matthews, 20 Dec. 1808, John Cook sec.
Harris, Robert & Mary White, 10 Jan. 1791, William White sec.
Harris, Sherwood & Joannah Ragsdale, 25 Oct. 1800, Robert Ragsdale
sec.
Harris, Thomas & Elizabeth Graves, 28 Dec. 1795, Peter Elam sec.
Harris, William & Mary I. Elam, 27 Sept. 1799, David Wilson sec.
Note from Barkley Elam, father of Mary - wit. Jos.Townes.
Harris, William H. & Chary Hudson, 14 June 1802, William Hudson
sec.
Harris, William & Anna Reamy, 12 Nov. 1804, Abraham Reamy sec.
Note from James Reamy, father of Anna.

Hasting, Absolom & Patsey Wade, 12 Jan. 1789, John Wagstaff sec.

Hastin, Henry & Fanny W. Graves, 19 June 1799, Thomas Graves sec.
Hastin, John & Nancy Ellin, 8 Oct. 1787, Absolom Hastin sec.

Hatsell, Edward & Sary Cox, 16 Mar. 1804, Stephen Hatsell sec.
Hatsell, John & Aggy Smith, 5 Apr. 1736, John Lollis sec.
Hatsell, John & Prudence Hetton, 17 Feb. 1786, W. Baskervill sec.
Hetsel, Stephen & Nancey Roberts, 12 Nov. 1792, Wm. Nanny sec.

Hawks, Joseph & Phebe Westbrook, 13 May 1799, Thomas Westbrook sec.

Hawkins, Claiborne & Margaret Barry, 2 May 1789, Frederick Andrews
          sec.
Hawkins, Green, & Mowning Carroll, 27 Dec. 1802, Mark Jackson sec.
Hawkins, John & Elizabeth Goode, 19 Dec. 1785, Robert Goode sec.
          Note from Edward Goode, father of Elizabeth
Hawkins, John D. & Jane A. Boyd, 11 Apr. 1803, Richard Boyd sec.
Hawkins, Phil, of North Carolina, & Lucy Davis, 22 Aug. 1775,
          William Davis sec.
Hawkins, Uriah & Lacy Green Jones, 17 Mar. 1798, William Jones sec.
Hawkins, William & Nancey Boyd, 12 Dec. 1803, Richard Boyd sec.

Hayes, Hyram & Phebe Hill, 8 Aug. 1791, Nicholas Jeter sec.
Hayes, James T. & Mary Puryear, 23 Dec. 1791, Reuben Puryear sec.
Hayes, James & Patsey Green, 22 Mar. 1806, James T. Hayes sec.
          Note from W. W. Green, father of Patsey.
Hayes, John, Jr. & Catey Decker, 19 Aug. 1794, William Decker sec.

Haynes, George, of Charlotte, & Sarah Gregory, 9 Feb. 1795,
          Joseph Gregory sec.

Hayles, John & Mary Sullivant, 26 May 1783, W. Baskervill sec.
          Note from William Starling.

Hazlewood, Daniel & Lucy Waller, 2 Aug. 1803, John Waller sec.

Heathercock, Whittemore & Henrietter Ladd, 26 Nov. 1808, James
          Drumright sec.

Hearn, John & Elizabeth Hill Whilbey, 18 Dec. 1793, Nathaniel
          Chambers sec. Note from Masey Crowder, mother of
          Elizabeth.

Heggie, John & Mary Ann Hunt, 29 Aug. 1807, Absolom Hunt sec.
          Note from James Hunt, father of Mary Ann.

Hendrick, John & Edith King, 25 Oct. 1800, Henry King sec.
Hendrick, Thomas & Salley Wall, 12 Dec. 1803, Charles Hamblin sec.
Hendrick, William & Susannah Crews, 8 Mar. 1778, John Atkinson
          sec.
Hendrick, William & Rebecka Wall, 11 Feb. 1805, Howel Graves sec.

Hepburn, William & Mary Watts McHarg, 12 Sept. 1785, George
          Tarry sec.

Hester, Francis & Ann Greenwood, 13 Dec. 1779, James Hester sec.
    Note from Thomas Greenwood, father of Ann.
Hester, James & Elizabeth Hix, 4 Sept. 1767, Amos Hix sec.
Hester, Robert & Nancy Locket, 13 Feb. 1792, John Wilson sec.
Hester, Robert & Mary Crowder, 29 July 1795, Robert Hester,Sr. sec.
Hester, Robert & Susannah Garner, 11 Jan. 1802, Richard Swepson sec.
Hester, Robert & Lucy Culbreath, 12 Jan. 1807, John Farrar sec.
Hester, Samuel & Elizabeth Greenwood, 8 Nov. 1784, Caleb Johnston
    sec. Note from Thos. Greenwood, father of Elizabeth.

Hicks (Hix), Ben, of Chesterfield Co., S. C. & Lucy Brooking, 15
    June 1786, William Lucas sec.
Hicks, Daniel & Fanney Delony, 18 Sept. 1788, William Delony sec.
Hicks, David & Nancey Thompson, 23 Jan. 1795, George Thompson sec.
Hicks, Isaac & Frances Lucas, 10 Mar. 1807, John R. Lucas sec.
Hicks, Jacob & Jincey Gordan, 31 Oct. 1794, Arthur T. Winfield sec.
Hicks, John & Gracey Coleman, 22 June 1789, Pettus Phillips sec.

Hightower, Devernix & Susannah Hutcheson, 18 Aug. 1800, Joseph
    Hutcheson sec. Note of Charles Hutcheson, father of
    Susannah.
Hightower, Stephen, & Tabitha Baugh, 16 July, 1808, Richard Baugh
    sec.

Hilton, William & Jincey Hutt, 10 Feb. 1800, Thomas Hutt sec.

Hill, Edward & Jemimah Blankenship, 28 July 1802, John Webb sec.
Hill, John & Elizabeth Marshall, 20 Feb. 1799, John Dortch sec.
    Note of Robert Marshall, father of Elizabeth, wit. Traverse
    Barber & Thomas Marshall.
Hill, Richard & Nancy Phillips, 29 Jan. 1800, William Brown sec.
    Note from Dabney Phillips, father of Nancy - wit. William
    Dodson.
Hill, Richard & Salley Burnett, 17 July 1806, Jesse Burnett sec.
Hill, William & Ann Freeman (Wagstaff?), 8 June 1789, Britain
    Wagstaff sec.

Hinton, Presley & Elizabeth Worsham, 10 Jan. 1801, William Blanton
    sec.

Hite, Vincent & Nancey Wilborn, 14 Dec. 1807, Thomas Wilborn sec.
    Note from John Wilborn, father of Nancey.

Hix (Hicks) Daniel & Susannah Jeffries, 12 Apr. 1784, John Jeff-
    ries sec.
Hix, Jesse & Sarah Bugg, 26 Nov. 1774, Samuel Bugg sec.
Hix, Nathaniel, of Georgis, & Frances Burton, 9 Oct. 1783, Sher-
    wood Bugg sec.
Hix, Sherwood & Ann Gordan, 18 Jan. 1782, Walter Leigh sec.
Hix, Thomas & Elizabeth Belville, 13 Dec. 1796, Francis Neal sec.

Hodge, John & Jane Thornton, 24 Oct. 1787, Hugh B. Nanny sec.

Holt, Thomas, of Chesterfield Co. & Charlotte Blackbourn, 12 Oct.
1780, John Brown sec.
Holt, Thomas B. & Jane Field, 25 May 1802, John Dortch sec.

Holmes, Daniel & Creasy Seward, 1 Jan. 1810, Samuel Vaughan, sec.
Holmes, David, & Elizabeth Clark, 15 Jan. 1790, Sam Thompson, Jr.
sec.
Holmes, Edards & Elizabeth Allen, 17 June 1797, James Jones sec.
Holmes, John & Mary Taylor, 20 Dec. 1779, Jones Taylor sec.
Holmes, John & Milley Turner, 31 Aug. 1797, Matthew Turner sec.
Note from John Turner, father of Milley.
Holmes, Pennington & Rebecca Daws, 29 June 1798, John Daws sec.
Holmes, Samuel & Prudence Courtney, 23 Oct. 1775, William Turn-
bull sec.
Holmes, Sam & Hannah Fox, 13 Dec. 1796, Edward Holmes sec.
Holmes, William & Betsey Crowder, 25 Feb. 1783, Charles Davis sec.

Holloway, Anderson & Susanna Gillispie, 1 July 1799, John Dortch sec.
Holloway, David, & Mary Wright, 21 Dec. 1799, John Holmes sec.
Holloway, Edward & Nancy Farrar, 8 Nov. 1806, Francis Ballard sec.
Holloway, George & Anne Hall, 24 Oct. 1774, William Holloway sec.
Note from James Hall, father of Anne
Holloway, Gray & Maryanna Baker, 24 Jan. 1801, William Holloway sec.
Holloway, John & Ann Starling, 17 Dec. 1793, Richard Hanserd sec.
Note from William Starling, father of Ann.
Holloway, John & Frances Crowder, 12 Jan. 1795, Godfrey Crowder sec.

Hood, Charles & Sarah Durham, 28 June 1786, James Willis sec.
Hood, John & Salley Rudd, 8 Oct. 1804, William Burchett sec.
Hood, Sterling & Martha Vaughan, 11 July 1785, George Barnes sec.
Note from Robert Hood, father of Sterling.

Hooper, John & Mary Tanner, 7 July1806, Benj. Beekes sec.

Hopkins, Edmund & Martha Cary Jones, 25 July 1796, John Dortch &
W. Baskervill sec. Note from Tignal Jones, father of
Martha.
Hopkins, Samuel & Betty Bugg, 18 Jan. 1783, George Nicholas sec.

Hord, James & Martha Puryear, 14 Nov. 1803, Thomas Thompson sec.
Hord, Jesse & Mary C. Erskin, 12 Feb. 1798, William Christopher sec.
Hord, Thomas & Mary Camp, 26 Dec. 1785, John Holmes sec.

House, John & Salley Evans, 9 Apr. 1808, Labon Short sec. Note
from Elizabeth Evans, mother of Salley.
House, Marriott H., of Brunswick Co. & Polley Short, 23 Aug. 1790,
Miles House sec. Note from Jacob Short, father of Polley.
House, Miles, of Brunswick Co. & Salley Short, 23 Jan. 1788, John
Stegall sec. Note from Jacob & Mary Short, parents of
Salley.

Hudson, Benjamin & Salley Vaughan, 21 Mar. 1792, Thos. Chappell
Singleton sec. Note from Richard Vaughan, father of Salley.
Hudson, Charles & Nancy Goode, 18 Dec. 1790, Chiles Hutcheson sec.

Note from Joseph Goode, father of Nancy.
Hudson, Culbert & Lucy Goodwin, 24 Dec. 1784, William Goodwin sec.
    Note from Peter Goodwin, father of Lucy.
Hudson, David & Sarah Draper, 3 Dec. 1789, John Hudson sec.
Hudson, George & Molley Berry, 11 Dec. 1786, William Harris sec.
    Note from Thomas Barry, father of Molley.
Hudson, Hall & Dicy Allgood, 9 Nov. 1801, John Hudson sec.
Hudson, Jacob, & Sarah Wade, 8 Sept. 1788, William Lankester sec.
Hudson, James & Betsey Mullins, 1 Feb. 1786, Cox Whitton sec.
Hudson, John &,Rebecca Ezell, 26 Mar. 1794, Thomas Calvery sec.
Hudson, John & Salley Williams, 14 July 1800, Ch. Robertson sec.
Hudson, John & Fanny Bland, 30 Apr. 1801, Swepson Jeffries, Jr.
    sec. Note from Samuel Bland, father of Fanny.
Hudson, John & Lucy Tucker, 10 Dec. 1804, Richard Walden sec.
Hudson, Richard & Patsy Holloway, 14 Jan. 1805, Jordan Mason sec.
Hudson, Richard & Elizabeth Dodson, 30 July, 1810, Edwd. Dodson sec.
Hudson, Samuel & Nancy White, 8 Feb. 1790, William White sec.
Hudson, William & Taffanus Moore, 2 Mar. 1787, John Wagstaff sec.
Hudson, William & Jane Puryear, __ Nov. 1803, Peter Puryear sec.
Hudson, William & Elizabeth Keeton, 8 Oct. 1804, Richard Hudson sec.
Hudson, Young & Fanny Hutcheson, 9 July, 1804, John Pritchett sec.

Hughes, James & Frances Norment, 13 Mar. 1769, William Norment sec.
Hughes, Richard & Sally Christopher, 17 Aug. 1786, David Stokes.

Humphries, Benjamin & Mary Keeton, 25 Nov. 1788, Joseph Keeton sec.

Hume, Frederick & Elizabeth D. Butler, 12 Mar. 1804, John White sec.

Hundley (Hunley), Cyer & Ann Holmes, 26 July 1791, Sack Holmes sec.
Hunley, Willis & Joyce Lark Taylor, 23 Sept. 1809, Jones Taylor sec.

Hunt, James, of Charlotte Co. & Prudence Loafman, 26 Sept. 1801,
    William Graves sec.
Hunt, Jesse & Polly Wagstaff, 8 May, 1799, William Hunt sec.
Hunt, Moza & Salley Overton, 10 Nov. 1808, John Doggett sec.
Hunt, Samuel Goodwin & Martha Drumright, 20 Dec. 1802, William
    Drumright sec.
Hunt, William & Sarah Allgood, 28 July 1788, Will Johnson sec.

Hurt, James & Ermen Vaughan, 11 Sept. 1809, William Burton sec.
Hurt, William & Betty Hudson, 22 July, 1890, John Hudson sec.

Hutcheson, Chiles & Fanny Moss, 23 Dec. 1791, Note from Ray Moss,
    father of Fanny.
Hutcheson, John & Sarah Hutcheson, 22 Nov. 1786, Peter Hutcheson
    sec.   Note from Chas. Hutcheson, father of Sarah.
Hutcheson, John & Nancy Stone, 9 Dec. 1793, William Stone sec.
Hutcheson, John & Sarah Baugh, 23 Dec. 1793, James Baugh sec.
Hutcheson, John & Molley Suggett, 31 Aug. 1801, Samuel Hutcheson
    sec.
Hutcheson, Peter & Lilley Wagstaff, 11 Dec. 1797, John Wagstaff
    sec.
Hutcheson, Richard & Salley Turner, 24 Nov. 1798, Matthew Turner
    sec.

Hutcheson, Richard, Jr. son of John, & Wilmouth Turner, 11 Oct. 1804,
    Jacob Shelor sec.
Hutcheson, Samuel & Hannah C. Brame, 19 Oct. 1796, William Phillips
    sec. Note from James Brame, G'dn. of Hannah.
Hutcheson, William & Mary W. Brown, 13 Dec. 1790, Thomas Brown sec.

Hyde, John & Anne Walton, 16 Nov. 1786, Edward Walton sec.

Inge, Richard & Sarah Johnson, 7 Nov. 1785, William Davis sec.

Ingram, John & Sarah Collier, 7 June 1773, Charles Hutcheson sec.
Ingram, Samuel & Martha Vaughan, 25 Sept. 1792, William Green sec.

Iseman, Ludwick & Fanny Avery, 10 Nov. 1794, Harwood Rudd sec.

Ivy, Frederick & Prissey Stewart, 14 Dec. 1795, William Willis sec.

Jackson, Berkley & Martha Brown, 12 June, 1809, William Hutcheson sec.
Jackson, Birs & Polley Turner, 23 Apr. 1803, Drury Turner sec.
Jackson, Burwell & Nancy Thompson, 19 Nov. 1803, Drury Turner sec.
Jackson, Flemmen & Pattey Power, 9 Oct. 1792, Samson Power sec.
Jackson, Francis & Elizabeth Curtis, 2 May 1807, Samuel Simmons sec.
Jackson, Jaral & Mary Garrott, 13 Nov. 1798, Cavel Jackson sec.
    Note from Thomas Garrott, father of Mary.
Jackson, Mark Lambert & Druciller Rainey, 8 Nov. 1784, Francis Ray
    sec.
Jackson, Mark L. & Leannah Basey Webb, 3 July 1797, John Webb sec.
Jackson, Nathaniel & Nancy Turner, 24 Dec. 1804, W. Baskervill sec.
Jackson, Reuben & Annis Leagon, 10 Mar. 1800, John Walker sec.
Jackson, Tallg & Celey Epperson, 2 Oct. 1802, Henry Jackson sec.
Jackson, William & Nancy Bugg, 11 Sept. 1807, John Bugg sec.

Jarrott, Zachariah & Peggy M. Burton, 12 Apr. 1806, Jones Burton sec.

Jeffries, Archillis & Elizabeth Smith, 14 Sept. 1779, Drury Smith sec.
    Note from Eli Smith, father of Elizabeth.
Jeffries, Benjamin & Nancy Evans, 11 Dec. 1809, Matthew Baptist sec.
Jeffries, James & Ann Hogan, 11 May 1789, Lewis (James?) Toone sec.
Jeffries, John L. & Rebecca Richards, 8 Sept. 1806, William Richards
    sec.
Jeffries, Richard & Jane Whitehead, 1 July 1783, Robert Smith sec.
Jeffries, Richard & Prudence Russell, 19 June, 1797, Thomas Burnett
    sec.
Jeffries, Swepson, Jr. & Elizabeth Coleman, 6 Mar. 1788, W. Baskervill
    sec. Note from Swepson Jeffries, father of Swepson, Jr.
    wit. Thos. & Elizabeth Burnett & William Lewis.

Jeffries, Swepson & Isabell Goode, 8 Feb. 1789, Benj. Pennington sec.
Jeffries, Swepson & Sarah Minor, 10 Mar. 1800, George Minor sec.
Jeffries, Thomas & Mary Richeson, 26 Feb. 1798, James Harrison sec.
Jeffries, William B. & Elizth. Jeffries, 5 Oct. 1801, Richard Jeff-
    ries sec.

Jeter, Charles P. & Mary Phillips, 22 Dec. 1802, Williamson Pattillo
    sec. Note from Dabney Phillips, father of Mary.
Jeter, William & Lucy Speed, 11 Dec. 1780, Dabney Phillips sec.

Johnson, Allen & Polley Hutcheson, 12 Nov. 1792, Chiles Hutcheson sec.
Johnson, Archer & Nancy Dorthum, 14 May 1804, James Williams sec.
Johnson, Isaac & Rebecca Bowen, 30 Jan. 1802, Littleberry Bowen sec.
Johnson, Jacob & Linchey Crowder, 5 Feb. 1795, Edmond Burnett sec.
    Note from John Crowder, father of Linchey, wit. Roger Gregory,
    William Crowder & Edwd. L. Tabb, magistrate.
Johnson, James, & Elizabeth Russell, 30 Oct. 1780, Jeremiah Crowder
    sec.
Johnson, James & Salley Russell, 28 Feb. 1786, John Tisdale sec.
Johnson, James & Sarah Pettus, 10 Nov. 1794, Thomas Pettus sec.
Johnson, James & Sarah Cox, 12 Sept. 1796, Joseph Johnson sec.
Johnson, James & Patsey Reader, 14 Jan. 1799, Thomas Reader sec.
Johnson, John & Elith. Harrison, 11 Jan. 1802, Greenwood Harrison sec.
Johnson, John & Betsey Green Marshall, 22 Dec. 1802, Jordan McKinny
    sec. Note from Richard Marshall, father of Betsey, wit.
    Theophilus Marshall.
Johnson, John, of Charlotte Co. & Parmelia Mayne, 10 Dec. 1804,
    Samuel Weatherford sec. - Note from James Mayne, father of
    Parmelia.
Johnson, Michal & Salley Carter, 10 Dec. 1781, John Johnson sec.
Johnson, Phillip & Polley Stainback, 24 Jan. 1794, D. Wilson & W.
    Baskervill sec. Note from Laura Stainback, mother of
    Polley.
Johnson, William Whitehead & Mira Parson Scott, 29 July 1793 -
    Note from Will Johnson, father of William Whitehead.

Jones, Benjamin & Linne Pierce, 10 June 1803, Richard Jones sec.
Jones, Benjamin & Jane S. Coleman, 12 Dec. 1808, William Coleman
    sec.
Jones, Cleten & Parthene Crew, 13 July 1807, Ruel Allen sec.
Jones, Daniel & Martha Hamblin, 13 Mar. 1792, T. Vaughan sec.
Jones, Darling & Keziah Blacketer, 21 Mar. 1798, Will Jones sec.
Jones, Edward & Sarah Butler, 9 July 1792, Elijah Graves sec.
Jones, Francis & Nancy Booth, 18 Sept. 1799, Harper Booth sec.
    Note from Thomas Booth, father of Nancy.
Jones, Frederick & Nelly Brooks, 16 Oct. 1787, Jurdain Brooks sec.
    Note from Robert Brooks - wit. John & Carrel Jones.
Jones, Harwood & Rachel Crenshaw, 20 Oct. 1809, G. H. Baskervill
    sec. Note from Thomas A. Jones.
Jones, James & Elizabeth Holmes, 20 Dec. 1790, Pennington Holmes
    sec.
Jones, James & Nancy Robertson, 13 Oct. 1794, James Hudson sec.
Jones, James & Ann Hunt, 13 Mar. 1804, Philemon Hunt, Jr. sec.
Jones, James B. & Jane J. Davis, 3 Aug. 1810, G. H. Baskervill sec.
Jones, John & Judith Booth, 22 Jan. 1807, Harper Booth sec.
Jones, Joseph & Ann B. Rogers, 7 Dec. 1807, James Whitlow, Jr. sec.
Jones, Peter & Sarah Jackson, 11 Dec. 1797, Jeremh Clanch sec.
Jones, Richard & Nancy Hamblin, 23 Feb. 1799, Daniel Jones sec.
    Note from Thomas Hamblin, father of Nancy.
Jones, Robert & Mary Morgan, 14 Dec. 1795, Samuel Puryear sec.

Jones, Robert H. & Elizabeth Baskervill, 9 Apr. 1807, Robert Park sec.
Jones, Robert & Betsey Ann Jackson, 8 Dec. 1810, Mark L. Jackson sec.
Jones, Robert & Betsey Guy, 8 Aug. 1809, Daniel Guy sec.   Note
      from Lucy Guy, mother of Betsey.
Jones, Samuel & Dosha Haley, 9 Mar. 1789, Daniel Jones sec.
Jones, Thomas & Nancy Winfield, 26 Nov. 1787, Joshua Winfield sec.
Jones, Thomas A. & Mary Crenshaw, 18 Dec. 1799, James Jones sec.
Jones, Tignal & Sarah Anderson, Spinster, 16 Nov. 1767, Tignal Jones,
      Jr. sec.
Jones, William & Susanna Clark, 26 Dec. 1792, John Hudson sec.
Jones, William & Charity Jackson, 22 Oct. 1794, John M. Carter sec.
Jones, William & Lucy Lockett, 14 Dec. 1801, James Wilson sec.
Jones, William &Patsey B. Rogers, 8 Dec. 1810, Joseph Jones sec.
Jones, Willis, & Polley Stone, 4 Nov. 1803, William Stone sec.

Jordan, Miles & Harriott Pettus, 12 Nov. 1804, John Pettus sec.
      Note from W. Pettus, brother of Harriott.

Keeton, John, son of Joseph, & Nancy Allgood, 5 May 1792,
      William Westbrook sec.   Note from Moses Allgood, father of
      Nancy - wit. Anne Kirkland.
Keeton, Joseph & Sarah Cheatham, 8 Aug. 1803, Warner Keeton sec.
Keeton, Joseph & Betsey Moore, 13 Oct. 1806, Joseph Johnson sec.
Keeton, Leonard & Polley Tucker, 10 Nov. 1794, Daniel Tucker sec.
Keeton, Leonard & Mary Tucker, 9 Mar. 1801, Thomas Coley sec.
Keeton, Thomas & Nancy Bing, 13 Nov. 1805, James Keeton sec.
Keeton, Warner & Lucy Mason, 13 Feb. 1804, William Stone sec.
Keeton, William & Elizabeth Bing, 12 Nov. 1798, Note from George
      Bing, father of Elizabeth

Keen, Abraham & Margaret Tabb, 29 Dec. 1790, Edwd. L. Tabb sec.

Kelly (Kelley), Abner & Polley Lanier, 23 Feb. 1798, John Flagins
      sec.
Kelley, Francis & Delilah Crowder, 25 May 1785, W. Baskervill sec.
      Note from George Crowder, father of Delilah.
Kelley, Henry, of Brunswick Co. & William Nanney, 13 Mar. 1793.
      William Nanny sec.
Kelley, John & Frances Crowder, 6 Dec. 1804, Charles Kelley sec.

Kennon, Erasmus & Nancy Carter Nelson, 14 Nov. 1808, George
      Craghead sec.
Kennon, Richard, of Chesterfield Co. & Elizabeth Beverley Munford,
      16 May 1780, William Randolph sec.   Note from Robert
      Munford, father of Elizabeth - wit. John Vandyck & Will-
      iam Bridgwater.

Kendrick, James & Elizabeth Wright, 12 Dec. 1797, John Wright sec.

Kidd, James & Frances Robertson, 8 Aug. 1795, Mark Robertson sec.
Kidd, William & Judy Carter, 8 Oct. 1781, Lemon Williams sec.

King, Henry, of Brunswick Co. & Sarah Taylor, 18 July 1804, James
  Minge Thompson sec.
King, James & Sarah Morgan, dau. Reuben Morgan, 27 Mar. 1779, Reuben
  Morgan sec.
King, Capt. Miles, of Norfolk, & Frances Burwell, 15 July 1799, W.
  Baskervill sec.   Note from John S. Ravencroft, as to Capt.
  Miles, & from Ann Burwell, mother of Frances.

Kirks (Kirk), Charles & Mary Persize, 10 Nov. 1787, Joseph Mason sec.
Kirk, William & Ann Parham, 8 July 1788, Lewis Parham sec.
Kirks, William & Jane Arnold, 26 Jan. 1790, William McCan sec.
  Note from Samuel Kirks, father of William.

Kirkland, George & Martha Johnson Stainback, 29 June 1809, Phillip
  Johnson sec.

Knight, William & Elizabeth Oliver, 16 Oct. 1799, Richard Oliver
  sec.

Ladd, Amos & Elizabeth Crowder, 15 Oct. 1792, John Ladd sec.
Ladd, John & Jincey Cleaton, 17 Dec. 1798, Joseph Ladd sec.
Ladd, Noble & Mary Rottenberry, 29 Dec. 1792, John Ladd sec.
Ladd, Thomas, Jr. & Mary Crowder, __ Aug. 1788, Josiah Floyd sec.
Ladd, William & Martha Gillum, 8 Feb. 1787, Jacob Ladd sec.
Ladd, William & Fatha Pennington, 29 Dec. 1800, John T. Pennington.
  sec.   Note from Henry Pennington, father of Fatha.

Laffoon, Nathaniel & Polly Merryman, 18 Dec. 1804, John Nash sec.
Laffoon, Nathaniel & Mary Chamblous, 17 Nov. 1808, George Small
  sec.

Laine, Benjamin & Patsey M. Mayne, 10 Nov. 1800, Owen Lowry sec.
  Note from James Mayne, father of Patsey.

Lamkin, Cleophas & Mary Doggett, 19 Dec. 1785, James Garner sec.
  Note from John Doggett, father of Mary - wit. Edward Finch
  & James Norman.

Lambert, Ezekiel & Biddy Roberts, __ Feb. 1804, Robert Roberts sec.
Lambert, Isham & Salley Blanton, 17 June, 1796, James Burton sec.
Lambert, John & Jemimah Jackson, 2 Aug. 1785, Joseph Lambert sec.
Lambert, John & Elizabeth Gregory, 11 Dec. 1809, William Vaughan
  sec.   Note from Richard Gregory, father of Elizabeth.
Lambert, Julias & Jinsey Brooks, 13 Dec. 1796, John McKinney sec.
  Note from Robert Brooks, father of Jinsey.
Lambert, Thomas & Francis Wilson, 18 Apr. 1797, Richard Stone sec.
Lambert, William & Sarah Bottom, 31 May 1800, James Burton sec.

Lanier, Allen & Polley Davis, 21 Nov. 1791, Josiah Floyd sec.
  Consent from Charles & Martha Floyd for Polley Davis.
Lanier, Nicholas & Sarah Bugg, 28 Mar. 1796, John Nance sec.
Lanier, William & Mary Garland Ballard, 4 Sept. 1794, James
  Bullock, of Granville Co., S.C. sec. Note from John
  Ballard, father of Mary.

Langley, John & Lucy Young, 5 Dec. 1798, Allen Young sec.
Langley, Thomas & Joyce Bugg, 24 Apr. 1773, Samuel Hopkins, sec.
Langley, Walter & Judith B. Young, 5 Nov. 1803, Jesse Dortch sec.
    Note from Allen Young, father of Judith.

Leagan, James & Hannah Christopher, 11 Oct. 1796, John Leagan sec.
Leagan, James & Anne Gregory, 14 Nov. 1798, James Reamy sec.

Leach, James, Jr. & Patsey Gregory, 18 Jan. 1802, Francis Gregory
    sec. Note from Roger Gregory, father of Patsey.

Lee, Amos & Elizabeth Thompson, 13 Nov. 1809, Morgn. Thompson sec.
Lee, Jesse & Elizabeth Northington, 3 Dec. 1803, Samuel Butler sec.

Leigh, Anselm, of Richmond Co., Ga. & Salley Greenwood, 20 Jan.
    1790, Walter Leigh, of Georgia, sec. Note from Thomas
    Greenwood, father of Salley, wit. John Monroe.
Leigh, Walter & Patty Holmes, 1 Dec. 1784, Samuel Holmes sec.

Lett, Francis & Elizabeth Thompson, 21 Sept. 1797, James Lett &
    John Thompson sec.
Lett, Hardeway & Mary Burton, 1 Sept. 1806, Pennington Lett sec.
Lett, Joseph, Jr. & Polly Jeffries Burnett ___ Jan. 1804,
    Matthew H. Davis sec. Note from Thomas Burnett, father
    of Polly.
Lett, Pennington & Frances Pennington, 14 Feb. 1810, John T.
    Pennington sec. Note from Josiah Floyd, G'dn. of Frances.
Lett, Robert & Suckey Burrus Lett, 17 Apr.1794, Wm.Parrish sec.
Lewis, Abraham & Louise Averet, 11 Feb. 1805, C. Granderson
    Feild sec.
Lewis, Abraham & Elizabeth Clark, 8 Oct. 1804, James Parham sec.
Lewis, Charles & Mary Anderson, 8 Nov. 1779, Howell Taylor sec.
Lewis, Edward & Elizabeth Clark, 10 Aug. 1807, Overton Wiles sec.
Lewis, Francis & Elizabeth Hester, 27 Apr. 1786, Henry Landefer sec.
Lewis, James & Susannah Anderson,25 June 1774,Thomas Anderson sec.
Lewis, Robert, of Granville Co., S. C. & Ann Bugg, 10 Nov. 1788,
    Samuel Bugg sec.
Lewis, Robert & Elizabeth Jones, 25 Feb. 1794, Asa Thomas &
    Francis Jones sec. Note from Tignal Jones, father of
    Elizabeth.
Lewis, Robert & Nancy Willis, 22 Aug. 1797, Edwd. Willis sec.
    Note from Edward Lewis, father of Robert & W. Willis,
    father of Nancy.
Lewis, Robert & Charlotte Butler, 8 Jan. 1810, Jones Allen sec.
Lewis, Thomas & Elizabeth Burchett, 22 Mar. 1806, John Dortch
    sec.

Lipford, John & Little Jones, 3 Dec. 1796, Buchner Whittemore sec.

Lisk, William & Dicy Eastham, 21 Dec. 1803, Richard Crowder sec.

Lockett, Francis & Martha Goode Marshall, 8 Mar. 1802, Valentine
    McCutcheon sec. Note from William Marshall, father of
    Francis.
Lockett, Royall & Prudence Clay, 20 Aug. 1789, James Elam sec.

Note from Charles & Phebe Clay, parents of Prudence - wit.
Dyer Phillips & John White.

Lollis, John & Aggy Spurlock, 5 Apr. 1786, John Hatsell sec.

Lonnon, Henry & Mary Elam, 13 Dec. 1802, Philip Ryon sec.

Love, William & Susanna Brame, dau. Thomas Brame, 6 May, 1803,
Ingram Roofe sec.

Lucas, Frederick & Martha Baskervill, 27 Oct. 1779, W. Baskervill sec.
Lucas, George & Patty Arnold, 21 Mar. 1770, James Arnold, sec.
Lucas, Dr. John R. & Hannah H. Brown, 26 Apr. 1806, John Dortch sec.
Note from R. Watson, G'dn. of Hannah.

Lumsden, John & Elizabeth Eastland, 8 Feb. 1788, Robert White sec.

Lumpkin, Anthony & Polley Yancey, 14 Nov. 1808, Charles Yancey sec.

Luny, Richard & Elizabeth Cook, 18 Jan. 1804, Herbert Cook sec.

Lunsford, Moses & Mary Fox, 28 Jan. 1796, John McKiny sec. Note
from Richard Fox, father of Mary - wit. Edward Pennington,
Jas. Blanton & Charles Coppidgie.

McCarter, James & Liza Bowen, 3 Dec. 1804, James Bowen sec.
McCarter, Thomas & Caty Bowen, 23 June 1803, James Bowen sec.

McCutcheon, Charles & Prudence Evans, 11 Dec. 1798, Richard
Jeffries sec.
McCutcheon, Valentine & Anna Hester, 10 Mar. 1800, Richard Brown
sec.

McDaniel, William & Rhody Mason, 11 Aug, 1795, Ezekiel Redding sec.

McGowan (see Macgowan)

McKenney (Mackinney) John & Elizabeth Douglas, 24 Dec. 1792,
David Thomas sec. Note from S.Douglas, father of Elizabeth.
McKenney, Willie & Mary Glover, 25 Feb. 1801, William Blanton sec.

McLin, Thomas & Delilah Evans, 23 Dec. 1794, John Guy sec.
McLin, William, of Greenville Cp. & Anne Venable __ Apr. 1801,
James McLin sec.

McQuay, William & Sarah Brooks, 11 Jan. 1785, Burwell Russell sec.

Mabry, Stephen & Tabitha Nance, 19 Apr. 1775, John Cook sec. -
Note from Isham Nance, father of Tabitha.

Mackinney (McKenney), Munford & Patsey Morgan, 10 Dec. 1789, John
Morgan sec.
Macgowan, Ebenezer & Frances Baugh, 28 July,1797,James Bough sec.

Madkins, William Durham & Jane Bailey, 9 Dec. 1793, H. Bailey sec.

Malone, Drury & Penelope Taylor, 14 June, 1774, Lewis Parham sec.
Malone, Frederick & Susannah Bilbo, 24 May 1774, John Bilbo sec.
Malone, Frederick & Judith Puckett, 19 May 1779, John Puchett, of
    North Carolina, sec.
Malone, George & Sarah Fowlks, 23 Oct. 1804, Gabriel Fowlks sec.
Malone, Isaac & Ann C. Courtney, 22 Sept. 1790, Josiah Floyd sec.
Malone, Isaac & Lucy Lowberry, 24 Mar. 1795, Joseph Walker sec.
Malone, Nathaniel & Elizabeth Evans, 31 May 1777, Note from Stephen
    Mabry, father of Elizabeth - wit. John & Ludwell Evans.

Mallet, Thomas & Betsey H. Allgood, __ Feb. 1804, George Allgood
    sec.

Manning, Benjamin & Fanney Guy, 5 May 1796, Laibe Chavous sec.

Marshall, Burnett & Lucy Wilson, 13 Oct. 1803, Frederick Watkins
    sec. - Note from Joseph Wilson, father of Lucy.
Marshall, Dennis & Frances Harper , 27 Aug. 1792, John Harper sec.
Marshall, Francis & Jane Hester, 7 Nov. 1803, Daniel Johnson sec.
    Note from Samuel Hester, father of Jane.
Marshall, Isaiah & Elizth. Winn, 17 Feb. 1802, Banister Winn sec.
Marshall, Sack & Salley Finn, 23 May 1795, David Bennington sec.
Marshall, Thomas & Elizabeth L. Baptist, 1 Mar. 1802, John G.
    Baptist sec. Note from Wm. G. Baptist, father of
    Elizabeth.
Marshall, William & Rebeccah Evans, 17 Dec. 1803, Matthew Evans sec.

Marable, John & Lucy R. Billups, 12 Dec. 1791, John Billups sec.
Marable, William & Frances Christopher, 1 Dec. 1801, Jesse Hord sec.

Martin, James & Dolley Ridley, 8 June 1789, Samuel Puryear sec.
Martin, James & Margaret Allen, 12 Mar. 1800, John Puryear, Jr. sec.
Martin, John & Betsey Coppedge, 3 Apr. 1799, Charles Coppedge sec.
Martin, John & Cary Crowder, 30 May 1797, Phileman Hurt, Jr. sec.
Martin, Oliver & Elizabeth Allen, 13 Mar. 1799, Richard M. Allen
    sec.
Martin, Warner & Martha Bailey, 6 Oct. 1783, Benj. Ferrell sec.
    Note from William Bailey, father of Martha.

Mason, Jordan & Agnes Walker, 10 Oct. 1808, Allen Walker sec.
Mason, Robert & Martha Johnson, 31 Mar. 1797, John Edwards sec.
Mason, William & Susanna Campbell, 14 Jan. 1795, Benj. Fargeson,Jr.
    sec.
Mason, William W. & Nancy Crenshaw, 9 Sept. 1805, G. H. Baskervill
    sec.

Massey, Peter & Hannah Wells, 11 Mar. 1802, William Garratt sec.
Massey, Thomas & Peggy Barry, 24 Apr. 1799, James Johnson sec.

Matthews, Enos & Liddy Overbey, 17 Sept. 1788, Richard Thompson
    sec.

Matthews, John, of Brunswick Co. & Martha W. Jordan, 18 Dec. 1799,
      Wilkins Ogburn sec. Note from Mary Jordan, mother of Martha.
Matthews, Thomas & Betsey Wilkerson, 22 Mar. 1809, John Rany sec.

Mayes, Bos. & Mary Neal, 13 ____ 1783, William Hundley sec.   Note
      from William Neal, father of Mary.
Mayes, Bozeman & Polly Neal, 10 Nov. 1783, William Neal sec.
Mayes, John & Elizabeth Hamblin, 7 Jan. 1789, John Wynn sec.
Mayes, William & Creecy Cox, 26 Dec. 1806, Miles Hall sec.

Mayo, Cuffey & Celey Stewart, 2 Apr. 1802, Daniel Mayo sec.
Mayo, Hutching & Sally Stewart, 10 Feb. 1806, Daniel Mayo sec.
Mayo, Pompy & Nancy Marks, 17 Dec. 1801, Mingo Mayo sec.

Maynard, Wagstaff & Fanney Hoard, 10 Dec. 1792, James Hord sec.

Mayne, James & Sarah Tibbs, 8 Mar. 1779, William Tibbs sec.

Mealer, Nicholas & Tabitha Ragsdale, 12 July 1802, Jas. Wilson sec.
Mealer, Phillip & Patty Jones, 14 May 1781, Jesse Sanders sec.
      Note from Thomas Jones, father of Patty.
Mealer, William & Nancy Humphries, 11 Sept. 1775, John Humphries
      sec.
Mealer, William & Elizabeth P. Puryear, 9 Nov. 1807, Thomas Lewis
      sec.

Meariman (Merriman), Epps & Amey Kirks, 26 Jan. 1790, James McCan
      sec.
Meariman, Eppa & Elizabeth Thomerson, 5 Jan. 1803, William Thom-
      erson sec.

Medley, Bartholomew & Salley Holloway, 23 Dec. 1797, Benj. Fer-
      guson sec.
Medley, Joseph & Elanner White, 10 Jan. 1807, John Dortch sec.

Merriman (Meariman), Isham & Luerelia Turner, 4 Apr. 1787, Abram
      Merriman sec.

Merritt, Thomas & Elizabeth Suggett, 14 Dec. 1785, Pennington
      Holmes sec. Note from Edgcomb Scoggett, father of
      Elizabeth.

Meredith, Joseph N. & Mary Baptist, 12 May 1800, G. H. Baskervill
      sec.

Mills, Charles & Juncey Baker, 9 Dec. 1799, Geo. Baker sec.
Mills, John & Susanna Pool, 27 Nov. 1808, Robert Greenwood sec.

Miller, Henry & Elizabeth Smith, 17 June, 1800, Zachariah Curtis
      sec.

Mitchell, Benjamin & Mary Stone, 14 Dec. 1795, William Stone sec.
Mitchell, Gideon & Salley Wagstaff, 7 Feb. 1804, Allen Wagstaff
      sec.

36

Mitchell, Ishmael & Elizabeth Nance, 6 Jan. 1808, Isham Nance,Jr. sec.
Mitchell, Reuben & Ann Pennington, 2 Apr. 1783, Edward Pennington sec.
Mitchell, Thomas & _____ Malone, 3 Aug. 1785, John Burton sec.
Mitchell, Thomas & Fanney Pulley, 31 Oct. 1810, William Daly sec.
Mitchell, William & Elizabeth Warren, 22 July 1786, Richard Stone, of
    Brunswick Co., sec.

Mize, Henry, of Brunswick Co. & Elizabeth Yeargen, 17 Jan. 1807, John
    Mize sec.
Mize, John & Lemenda Lambert, 24 Mar. 1795, Thomas Lambert sec.
Mize, John & Nancy Yeargen, 30 Dec. 1805, Jerry Mize sec.
Mize, Randolph & Martha Matthews, 28 Apr. 1798, Hudson Nipper sec.

Monroe, John & Margaret Culbreath, 10 Mar. 1789, Thomas Culbreath sec.

Montgomery, Richard P. & Sarah Hudson, 30 Jan. 1804, Richard Hudson
    sec.

Monday, Jesse & Judith Nash, 13 Nov. 1792, Moore Corner, of Halifax
    Co. sec.

Montague, Mickelburrough & Nancy Vaughan, 30 July 1798, Reuben
    Vaughan sec.
Moon, Joseph & Jane Johnson, 24 Jan. 1787, Isaac Johnson sec.
Moody, Arthur & Mary Hester, 13 Dec. 1796, James Palmer sec. Note
    from James Hester, father of Mary.
Moody, Francis & Patsey Vaughan, 14 Sept. 1789, William Moody sec.
    Note from Henry Moody, father of Francis.
Moody, Francis & Anna Hester, 26 Dec. 1805, Harwood Jones sec.
    Note from James Hester, father of Anna.
Moody, Henry & Polley Moody, 20 June 1793, Robert Hester sec. Note
    from Arthur Moody, father of Polley.

Moore, Feild & Sarah Lidderdil, 26 Nov. 1774, Thomas Moore sec.
    Note from Thomas Anderson, G'dn. of Sarah.
Moore, George & Elizabeth Moody, 14 July 1785, Thomas Moore sec.
Moore, John & Hannah Hutcheson, 11 Aug. 1801, Charles Hutcheson
    sec.
Moore, Philip,B. & Phebe Elam __ Dec. 1789, Peter Elam sec.
Moore, Robert & Nancy Harrison, 21 July 1796, John Ogburn sec.
Moore, Starling & Huldy Ladd, 27 Dec. 1799, Geo. Baker sec.
Moore, Warner & Betsey Edwards Northington, 6 May 1805, Robert
    Moore sec.
Moore, William, Jr. & Jane Williams, 8 Nov. 1787, William Moore,
    Sr. sec. Note from Elizabeth Williams, mother of Jane.

Morgan, Benj. & Mary Bilbo, 19 Dec. 1785, Fredk. Raney sec. Note
    from James Bilbo, father of Mary - wit. Nicholas Bilbo &
    John Morgan.
Morgan, John & Agnes Bilbo, 24 Aug. 1779, Joseph Bilbo sec. Note
    from James Bilbo, father of Agnes - wit. Matthew Bilbo.
Morgan, John, Jr. & Nancy Cox, 14 Mar. 1789, Philip Morgan, Sr.
    sec.
Morgan, John & Mary Pool, 17 Feb. 1790, Phil Morgan sec.

Morgan, John & Lucy Royster, 9 Mar. 1801, John Pritchett sec.
Morgan, John & Sarah Chamblin ____ 1803, Nathaniel Moss sec.
Morgan, Phil & Patty Puckett, 13 Oct. 1784, Fredk. Raney sec.
Morgan, Starling & Celia Loyd, 7 Aug. 1797, John Loyd sec.
Morgan, Starling & Martha Howard ____ Oct. 1802, Stephen Roberts sec.

Morris, Daniel & Nancy Saunders, 15 Dec. 1807, John Feagins sec.

     Note from John Saunders, Sr. father of Nancy.
Morris, Edward & Prudence Finn, 8 Feb. 1799, Nicholas Lanier sec.
Morris, Henry & Lucy Drumright, 15 Dec. 1807, William Drumright sec.
Morris, Jesse & Salley Drumright, 26 Jan. 1804, William Drumright
     sec.

Moss, John & Rebecca Cox, 11 Dec. 1809, Charles Cox sec.
Moss, Meredith, of Brunswick Co. & Nancy Osling, 21 May 1792,
     Samuel Osling sec. Note from Jesse Osling, father of
     Nancy.
Moss, Nathaniel & Helica Dortch, 8 Oct. 1777, Labon Wright sec.
Moss, Nathaniel & Martha Speed, 19 Apr. 1794, Lewis Dortch sec.
Moss, Ray & Jane Coleman, 16 Mar. 1782, William Coleman sec. Note
     from Richard Coleman.
Moss, William & James Stainback, 9 Dec. 1805, James Stainback sec.
     Note from Luise Stainback, mother of James?
Moss, William & Mary Robinson, 12 Oct. 1809, Henry Royall sec.

Mullins, Matthew & Elizabeth Crowder, 14 Sept. 1795, James Hudson
     sec.
Mullins, Valentine & Patsey Griggs, 10 Nov. 1794, James Hudson
     sec.

Murphey, William & Elizabeth Eppes, 8 May 1779, Isham Eppes sec.

Mustian, Jeffrey & Elizabeth Stegall, 5 Feb. 1787, James Chamblin
     sec.

Naish (Nash), Abraham & Polley Carter, 14 Nov. 1796, Wm.Naish sec.
Naish, William & Leliah Lett, 12 Oct. 1801, Thomas Hutt sec.

Nance, Daniel & Sarah Russell, 13 Mar. 1789, James Standley sec.
Nance, Isham, Jr. & Nancy Rainey, 8 Aug. 1803, Thomas Nance sec.
Nance, John & Frances Bugg, 10 Apr. 1786, Robert Nance sec.
     Note from John Bugg, father of Frances. wit. Sarah Bugg.
Nance, John & Frances Winn, 17 Mar. 1795, John Thomas sec.
Nance, Robert & Tabitha Pennington, 14 Jan. 1790, William Drum-
     right sec.
Nance, Thomas & Elizabeth Cleaton, 20 Dec. 1791, Thomas Cleaton
     sec.
Nance, Thomas & Eliza Giles, 4 Oct. 1795, John Cleaton sec.
Nance, Thomas & Salley Malone, 10 Jan. 1810, Thomas Cleaton sec.
Nance, William & Patsey Williams, 4 Feb. 1800.
Nance, Wyatt & Polley Cook, 9 Jan. 1794, John Cook sec.

Nanney, Hewbery & Patsey Roberts, 12 Jan. 1792, John Fowler sec.
    Note from William Roberts, father of Patsey.
Nanny, Roberts, & Sarah Morgan, 30 July, 1804, Starling Morgan sec.
    Note from Benjamin Morgan.
Nanny, William & Frances King, 5 May, 1806, Hughberry Nanny, sec.
    Note Lewis King, father of Frances.

Nash (Naish), John & Betsey Chambers, 16 Dec. 1795, Williamson
    Pattillo sec.
Nash, Wiley & Anne Pennington, 5 Jan. 1807, John Harper sec.
Nash, James & Tokey Pennington, 23 Dec.1786, Jno.Geo.Pennington sec.
Neal, Edward & Salley Green, 8 Dec. 1806, James T. Hayes sec.
Neal, John & Clarissa Poindexter, 9 Jan. 1775, Moses Overton sec.
Neal, Reaves & Elizabeth Worsham, 8 Oct. 1792, William Neal sec.
Neal, Thomas & Elizabeth Brown, 1 Jan. 1787, Thomas Brown sec.
Neal, Thomas & Elizabeth E. Coleman, 8 Oct. 1804, William Coleman
    sec.

Neblett, Sterling, Jr. & Ann Daly, 4 Oct. 1798, Charles Ogburn sec.
    Note from Josiah Daly, father of Ann.

Nelson, Norborne T. & Lucy Nelson, 8 Apr. 1805, Henry Young sec.
Nethery, Thomas & Ann Baker, 27 Jan. 1789, George Baker sec.
Newton, James & Elizabeth Newton, 14 Mar. 1803, Robert Newton sec.
Newton, Robert & Mary Read, 8 Sept. 1788, Elijah Graves sec.

Newsom, Robert & Martha Ruffin, 2 Oct. 1772, Francis Ruffin sec.
    Note from John Ruffin, father of Martha.

Nicholson, Starling & Elizabeth Moore, 5 July, 1802, Lewis Nichol-
    son sec.
Nicolson, William, of Henrico Co., & Martha Hardy, widow, 19 Nov.
    1786, Richard Swepson sec.

Nipper, Hutson & Frances Vaughan, 16 Nov. 1792, Ambrose Vaughan
    sec.
Nipper, Pace & Rody Vaughan, 23 Oct. 1793, Hudson Nipper sec.

Norment, James & Jane Jeffries, 28 June, 1793, Richard Jeffries
    sec.
Norment, Thomas & Ann Jeffries, 14 Feb. 1785, John Jeffries sec.

Northington, David & Martha Crowder, 13 Aug. 1804, Peter Crowder sec.

Northcross, William Renn & Frances Hatsell, 4 Mar. 1786, John
    McCarter sec.

Nowell, Allen & Elizabeth Stewart, 14 July 1800, Fredk. Nowell sec.
Nowell, John & Elizabeth Chamberlin, 22 Mar. 1785, John Hammer sec.
Nowell, Thomas & Salley Fox, 12 Oct. 1790, Thomas Roberts sec.

O'Briant, John & Patsy Moss, 14 Dec. 1795, William Moore sec.

Ogburn, Matthew & Sarah Daly, 15 Feb. 1792, Charles Ogburn sec. Note from Josiah Daly, father of Sarah.

Oliver, Asa & Sarah Wray, 1 Dec. 1772, John Oliver sec.
Oliver, James W. & Elizabeth Green, 2 Mar. 1799, Abraham Green sec.
Oliver, John & Elizabeth Bailey, 8 Dec. 1794, William Durham sec.
Oliver, Richard & Elizabeth Jeffries, 12 Dec. 1803, William Bilbo sec.
Oliver, Robert & Martha Moss, ___ Dec. 1805, Hy. Coleman sec.

Organ, Thomas & Sarah Lucas, 11 Nov. 1805, John Dortch sec.

Osborn, Jones & Nancy Fowlkes, 12 June 1797, Edward Elam sec.

Oslin, Isaac & Ann Pennington, 1 Mar. 1800, David Pennington sec.
Oslin, Samuel & Martha Bugg, 7 Mar. 1789, John Bugg sec.

Overbey, Jechonias & June Greenwood, 11 Jan. 1796, Hume R. Feild sec.
Overby, John & Elizabeth Childress, 11 June 1804, William Overbey sec. Note from Jinsy Childress, mother of Elizabeth.
Overbey, William & Susannah Yancey, 11 June 1804, Howel Graves sec.

Overton, John & Susannah Christopher, 10 Jan. 1772, William Christopher sec.
Overton, John & Elizabeth Ballard, 10 Nov. 1806, Francis Ballard sec.
Overton, Thomas & Martha Toone, 13 Apr. 1795, Edw. Hogan sec.
Overton, William S. & Mary Baskervill, 10 Dec. 1799, E. Baskervill sec.

Owen, Sherwood, of Halifax Co., & Salley Harris, 7 Nov. 1796, James Harris sec.

Palmer, Amasa & Sally Davis, 2 Mar. 1774, William Davis sec.
Palmer, Amasa & Judith Hendrick, 13 Dec. 1800, Christopher Haskins sec.
Palmer, James & Martha Hester, 9 May 1791, William Durham Madkins sec.
Palmer, William & Elizabeth Lewis, 12 Oct. 1772, Edward Lewis sec.

Parrish, Jesse & Elizabeth Hutcheson, 27 June 1810, John Ingram sec.
Parrish, William & Frances Lett, 30 Dec. 1786, Isaac Adams sec.
Parrish, William & Milla Tudor, 9 Dec. 180__, William Roberts sec.
Parrish, William & Martha Budd, 19 Nov. 1807, Augustin Smith sec.

Parham, Lewis & Betsey Bain, spinster, 22 May 1769, Jno.Tabb sec.

Patterson, Samuel & Sirily Poindexter, 11 Jan. 1773, Phil. Poindexter sec.

Pattillo, Samuel & Salley C. Phillips, 15 Dec. 1808, John C. Phillips sec. Note from Pettus Phillips.

Pattillo, Williamson & Jane Phillips, 13 July 1808, Martin Phillips
sec.

Patrick, John & Sarah Kindrick, 29 Sept. 1779, John Kindrick sec.

Paull, James & Elizabeth Brooks, spinster, 12 Feb. 1776, Dudley
Brooks sec.

Pearson, Littlebeary & Nanny Thomas, 1 Dec. 1786, Peter Thomas sec.
Pearson, Thomas & Mary Delony, 19 Sept. 1768, Henry Delony sec.

Peele, Edwin H. & Nancy Speed, 8 Jan. 1807, Chas. Ogburn sec. Note
from James Wilson, G'dn. of Nancy. - wit. Bob Speed.

Peebles, Thomas E. & Susanna P. Lucas, 20 Mar. 1804, William Parham
sec.

Pennington, Drury & Polly Quarles, 6 Dec. 1809, John Wright sec.
Pennington, Philip, & Patty Floyd, 29 Jan. 1787, John Saunders sec.
Pennington, Philip & Mary Burton, 31 May 1798, John Hubbard sec.
Pennington, Robert & Frances Finch, 26 Jan. 1787, Sherd. Smith sec.
Pennington, Walter & Polley Mabry, 22 Dec. 1802, Isham Nance,Jr.
sec.

Penticost, Scarbrough & Phebe Lockett, 8 Feb. 1790, Daniel Durham
Madkins sec.

Perkinson, Rowlett & Susanna Pettus, 19 Jan. 1798, Matthew Pettus
sec. Note from Wm. Stone - wit. Matthew Pettus & John
Hutcheson.
Perkinson, William & Mary Pettus, 8 Feb. 1790, Thos. Pettus sec.

Pettus, Horatio & Mary L. Poindexter, 9 Dec. 1799, Wm. Pettus sec.
Pettus, John & Elizabeth Walker Pettus, 12 Aug. 1782, Thos.Pettus,
Jr. sec.
Pettus, William & Betsey Ann Poindexter, 9 Mar. 1789, Samuel
Hopkins, Jr. sec.

Pettway, John, of Warren Co.,N. C. & Martha Alexander, 11 Aug.
1792, John Alexander sec.

Pettipool, W____? & Martha Ingram, 21 Dec. 1792, William Green
sec.
"Phillips" page 41
Pinson, Joseph & Mary Jones, 12 May 1794, Arthur Atkinson sec.
Note from Richard Jones, father of Mary.
Pinson, Thomas & Lucy Johnson, 12 Feb. 1810, Caleb Johnston sec.

Poarch,(Portch), Independance & Lucy Hudson, 8 Aug. 1801, Thomas
Webb sec.
Poarch, Isham & Nancy Matthews, 2 Jan. 1802, Benj. W. Hudson sec.

Poindexter, George & Nancy Hinton, 24 Dec. 1791, Randolph Westbrook sec.

Poindexter, Phillip & Janery Goode, 13 June 1768, Richard Wilton, Jr.
    sec. Note from Edward Goode, father of Janery.
Poindexter, Phillip & Mary Hinton, 12 Aug. 1799, Thomas Dance sec.

Pool (Poole), Alex & Angellice Crowder, 11 Oct. 1790, Thomas Norment
    sec.
Poole, Mitchel & Nancy Christopher, 16 Aug. 1797, Turner Sharp sec.
Poole, William & Rebecca Tanner, 17 Jan. 1797, Thomas Tanner sec.

Portch (Poarch), Independant & Patsey Ellis, 9 Feb. 1807, Morris
    Green Burton sec.

Potter, Abraham & Sarah Hawkins, spinster, 6 Feb. 1771, John Potter
    sec.
Potter, Donaldson & Jane Weight, 3 Sept. 1804, Edmund Clemments sec.

Powell, William & Lucindy Ramey, 21 Feb. 1810, Williams Cook sec.

Poythress, Lewis & Rebecca B. Taylor, 9 Apr. 1802, Thomas Watson sec.
Poythress, Lewis & Patsey Giles, 26 Dec. 1793, Meredith Poythress
    sec.
Poythress, Meredith & Edith Cleaton, 14 July 1781, William Cleaton
    sec.
Poythress, William & Ann Bently, 10 Nov. 1802, Thomas Rogers sec.

Preston, Joshua, of Brunswick Co. & Lishea Feagins, 18 Dec. 1792,
    John Saunders sec.

Pritchett, John & Susanna Cox, 14 Dec. 1795, William Hudson sec.
Pritchett, Thomas & Salley Hunt Hatsell, 7 Aug. 1798, Edwd. Hatsell
    sec.

Phillips, Archerbell & Mary Hanserd, 26 Nov. 1795, Richard Hanserd
    sec.
Phillips, Dabney, Jr. & Martha Hutcheson, 6 Jan. 1801, William
    Brown sec. Note from Dabney Phillips, father of Dabney, Jr.
    & from Charles Hutcheson, father of Martha.
Phillips, Dyer, & Patience Clay, 18 Dec. 1786, Thomas Dawson &
    John White sec. Note from Charles Clay, father of
    Patience.
Phillips, John, of Prince George Co., & Fanney Walker, 10 Sept.
    1798, Theophilus Feild, of Brunswick Co. sec.
Phillips, Jonathan & Martha Abenathy, 20 Dec. 1809, Liles Aben-
    athy sec.
Phillips, Martin & Lucy Suggett, 5 Nov. 1808, John Hutcheson sec.
Phillips, Pettus & Rebeccah Coleman, 6 Mar. 1788, Lewis Parham sec.
Phillips, William & Rachel Edmondson, 14 Oct. 1793, George B.
    Hamner sec. Note from Samuel Edmondson.
Phillips, William & Betsey Turner, 20 Dec. 1799, Matthew Turner
    sec.

Price, Pugh Williamson & Elizabeth Williamson, 4 July 1794,
    Isaiah Price sec. Note from Robert Williamson, father
    of Elizabeth.

Puckett, Banister, & Betsey Page, 7 Jan. 1801, Sack Bowen sec.
Puckett, John & Jane Jopkins, 28 Feb. 1792, John Farrar sec.

Pulley, James & Lucy Moss, 21 Dec. 1805, David Moss sec.
Pulley, William & Margaret Lowance, 26 Nov. 1784, Hubbard Ferrell sec.

Pulliam, Benj. & Ann Hester, 8 Mar. 1784, Stephen Mabry sec.
Pulliam, Byrd & Susanna Philips, 8 Apr. 1791, James Pulliam sec.
Pulliam, John & Elizabeth Wilson, 11 Sept. 1775, Benj. Pulliam &
    John Wilson sec.
Pulliam, Richard & Martha Mealer, 10 Oct. 1791, Elijah Graves sec.

Puryear, Elijah & Elizabeth Overton, 21 Dec. 1802, John Overton,
    Jr. sec.
Puryear, Hezh. & Kitty Hayes, 10 Jan. 1803, Thos. Puryear sec.
Puryear, James & Milley Mosely, 12 Dec. 1808, John Puryear sec.
Puryear, John & Johannah _____, 20 June, 178__, Samuel Puryear
    sec.
Puryear, John & Salley Clausel, 24 Oct. 1799, Hezekiah Puryear sec.
Puryear, John & Polly Hudson, 12 Dec. 1808, Samuel Hudson sec.
Puryear, Peter & Phebe Burton, 10 Dec. 1792, Thomas Crowder sec.
Puryear, Reuben & Martha Clausel, 23 Dec. 1791, James T.Hayes sec.
Puryear, Samuel & Frances Clausel, 17 Jan. 1786, Richard Clausel
    sec.
Puryear, Samuel & Salley Stith Puryear, 20 Sept. 1810, Mackentosh
    Puryear sec. Note from Sarah Puryear, mother of Salley.
Puryear, Seymour & Sarah Royster, 10 Apr. 1775, John Puryear sec.
Puryear, Seymour & Fanny Vaughan, 11 Mar. 1807, Wiley Burns sec.
    Note from Nancy Foster, Aunt of Fanny.
Puryear, Thomas & Patsey Harris, 25 Mar. 1801, Allin Harris sec.
    Note from Reubin Harris, father of Patsey.
Puryear, Thomas & Elizabeth Marshall, 13 May 1803, Francis
    Lockett sec.
Puryear, William & Rebecca Carleton, 22 Sept. 1785, John Farrar sec.
    Note from Thomas Carleton, father of Rebecca.

Quarles, Williamson & Polley Benford, 14 Jan. 1806, Thomas Benford
    sec.

Ragsdale, Anthony & Anne Wells, 1 Oct. 1793, William Westbrook sec.
Ragsdale, Cornelius & Frances Mealer, 5 Oct. 1795, William Hunley
    sec.
Ragsdale, Drury, & Susanna Mealer, 22 Dec. 1785, Thomas Wilbourn
    sec.
Ragsdale, Richard & Susanna Allen, 12 Nov. 1792, Robert Harris
    sec.
Ragsdale, Richard & Judith Hudson, 23 May 1799, Richeson Farrar
    sec.
Ragsdale, Richard & Barshaba Bishop, 8 Feb. 1802, Littleberry B.
    Carter sec.

Ragland, Abner & Nancy Fox, 3 Mar. 1799, Thomas Fox sec.

Ransom, James, of Amelia County & Mary Hayes, 9 July, 1787, James T.
Hayes sec.

Raney (Rainy-Rany-Rainey), Buckner & Rebecca Holmes, 12 June 1780,
Samuel Lark sec.
Rainey, Edmond & Polly H. Morgan, 21 Oct. 1807, Starling Morgan sec.
Rainey, Francis & Judith Lambert, 7 Jan. 1797, Mark Lambert Jackson
sec.
Raney, Fredk. & Molley Morgan, 10 May 1775, John Tabb sec.
Raney, Isham & Betsey Morgan, 20 Jan. 1789, Fredk. Raney sec.
Rainey, Robert & Levisy Crowder, 27 Mar. 1805, Nathaniel Crowder sec.
Rany, Smith & Ann Standley, 31 Dec. 1796, James Standley & Fredk.
Rainey sec.
Rainy, Williamson & Edith Morgan, 23 Nov. 1779, Francis Rainey sec.
Note from Reuben Morgan.

Ravenscroft, John Stark & Anne Spottswood Burwell, 13 Aug. 1792,
Will Hepburn sec.

Reader, Jake & Phebe Rubards, 13 July 1801, James Wilson sec.
Reader, Jept. & Winny Harrison, 10 Jan. 1803, Greenwood Harrison
sec.
Reader, Robert & Mary Mullins, 25 Dec. 1792, James Hudson sec.
Reader, Thomas & Lucy Mullins, 10 Dec. 1798, Rudd Hughes sec.

Reamy, Abraham & Susanna Hudson, 13 Mar. 1809, William Harris sec.
Reamy, Thomas A. & Phebe Burton, 13 Jan. 1800, James Wilson sec.

Reagan, John F. & Watharine Evans, 5 Oct. 1791, William Taylor sec.

Reams, Jeremiah & Dolly Fowler, 15 Dec. 1800, Starling Fowler sec.

Redding, Ezekiel & Rebecca Mason, 18 Apr. 1791, Thomas Marriott sec.

Reekes, Benj. & Lucy Ingram, 12 Aug. 1801, Richd. Crowder sec.
Reekes, James & Salley Holmes, 13 Dec. 1796, John Walton sec.

Richards, William & Mary Evans, 14 Dec. 1801, Richard Jeffries sec.

Ridout, Gordan & Salley Grigg, 6 Feb. 1802, William Ezell sec.
Note from Lewis Grigg, father of Salley.

Riggins, John & Mary Hutt, 14 May, 1798, William Hilton sec.

Rives, William & Mary Turner, 1 Jan. 1788, Nicholas Bilbo sec.
Note from Thomas Rives, father of William & from Stephen
Turner, father of Mary.

Roberts, Abraham & Susannah B. Collier, 3 Sept. 1807, Philip Roberts
sec.
Roberts, Anselm & Nancey Bottom, 22 July 1806, Huberry Nanny sec.
Roberts, Dennis & Lucy Roberts, 21 Dec. 1798, William Roberts sec.
Roberts, George & Polley Stembridge, 15 Oct. 1810, James Stem-
bridge sec.
Roberts, John & Leanner Allen, 21 May 1799, William Allen sec.

Roberts, Lewis & Siller May, 17 Oct. 1797, Henry Roberts sec.
Roberts, Philip & Tabitha Watson, 29 Dec. 1802, Thomas Shelton sec.
Roberts, Robert & Elizabeth Rook, 20 Feb. 1799, Starling Morgan sec.
Roberts, Stephen & Martha Gregory, 20 Aug. 1810, Nathaniel Fowlkes
    sec.
Roberts, William, Jr. & Frances Roberts, 21 Aug. 1802, Philip Roberts
    sec.

Robertson, Allen & Amasa Burrus, 4 Sept. 1801, Henry Royall sec.
Robertson, Drury & Mary Winfield, 4 Feb. 1786, Matthew Turner sec.
Robertson, John Moody & Mary E. Lamb, 1 Mar. 1792, Pines Ingram sec.
    Note from Joseph Boswell, G'dn. of Mary.
Robertson, Levderick & Nancy Thomas, 11 Mar. 1806, John Allgood sec.
Robertson, Nathaniel & Nancey Crews, 9 Dec. 1799, R. H. Watkins sec.
Robertson, Thomas & Elizabeth Roberts, 16 June 1787, Thomas Roberts
    sec.

Robinson, Clack & Elanor Young, 11 Oct. 1809, Walter Langley sec.
Robinson, James & Martha Winfield, 2 Nov. 1803, William Thomas sec.
    Note from Joshua Winfield, father of Martha.

Roffe, Edward & Miney Burton, 16 July 1787, Will Johnson sec. Note
    from Robert Burton, father of Miney.
Roffe, Ingram & Agniss Love, 17 Feb. 1803, William Love sec. Note
    from Charles Love, father of Agniss.
Roffe, John & Martha Simmons, 1 Jan. 1794, Samuel Simmons sec.
Roffe, Melchezedeck & Ann Dodson, 12 Dec. 1800, Wm. Dodson sec.
Roffe, William & Sarah Knight, 9 Oct. 1794, Ing. Vaughan sec.

Rose, Anderson & Polley Puryear, 9 July 1804, Valentine McCutcheon
    sec.

Ross, Robert & Lucy Arnold, 14 Nov. 1792, Elisha Arnold sec.

Rottenberry, Charles & Salley Glover, 4 Dec. 1798, James Burton sec.
Rottenberry, McDaniel & Nancy Bowen, 3 Mar. 1797, John Thomerson
    sec.
Rottenberry, Winn. & Elizabeth F. Hudgins, 26 Nov. 1801, Abel
    Edmunds sec. Note from James Hudgins, father of Elizabeth.

Rowland, Richard & Rachel Ragsdale, 10 Dec. 1781, Henry Hobertson
    sec.

Rowlett, Thompson & Polley Dodson, 9 Nov. 1805, Edward Dodson sec.

Royal, Henry & Pettey Hutt, 18 July 1805, Peter Puryear sec.

Royster, Charles & Elizabeth Burrows, 14 Nov. 1803, Jordan Mason
    sec. Note from W. T. Burrows, father of Elizabeth.
Royster, Clark & Lucy Apperson, 11 Oct. 1802, Archibald Clark sec.
Royster, Dennis & Rebecca Royster, 12 Jan. 1307, Stark Daniel sec.
Royster, Francis & Ann Roberts, 13 Dec. 1802, Valentine McCutcheon
    sec.
Royster, George & Susanna Hall, 7 Aug. 1790, William Marshall sec.
Royster, Henry & Frances Draper, 8 Nov. 1790, Joseph Royster sec.

Royster, Joseph & Elizabeth Draper, 12 Dec. 1791, Holeman Rice sec.
Royster, Wilkins & Mary Roberts, 13 Feb. 1797, Samuel Hester sec.

Rudd, John & Elizabeth Edmonson, 15 Oct. 1810, Brown Avory sec.

Rudder, Alexander & Elizabeth McLaughlin, 21 Dec. 1791, Edward Brodnax,
    of Lunenburg Co. sec.

Ruffin, Theodorick Bland & Susanna Murray, 14 Jan. 1788, Jesse Brown
    sec.   Note from William Yates - wit. Robt: Booth & G.Tucker.

Russell, Burwell & Prudence Hogan, 11 Jan. 1785, William McQuil sec.
Russell, Jeremiah, of Brunswick Co. & Jelley Akins, 26 Aug. 1795,
    James Atkins sec.
Russell, Jesse & Rachel Harris, 11 Dec. 1798, Stephen Evans sec.
Russell, John & Catherine Stone, 30 Mar. 1801, Benjamin Mitchell sec.
Russell, Mark & Mary Pucket, 3 Dec. 1785, John Daly sec.

Ryland, Jeason, & Lucy Dortch, 23 Feb. 1784, Nathaniel Moss sec.
Ryland, John & _____, 11 Jan. 1786, Thomas Addams sec.

Sadler, William & Avarilla Greenwood, 12 Nov. 1798, John Greenwood
    sec.   Note from Thomas Greenwood, father of Avarilla - wit.
    W. W. & Henry Pattillo.

Salley, James & Aubrey Keeton, 9 Dec. 1793, Reuben Carden sec.

Samnell, Andrew & Delina Tanner, 11 May 1786, Thomas Tanner sec.

Sanders, Benjamin & Mary Anne Moore, 19 Feb. 1791, Philip B. Moore
    sec.

Sandefer, Henry & Martha Taylor, 14 Dec. 1785, Samuel Durham sec.

Saunders, George & Halley Emery, 3 Dec. 1804, Thomas Saunders sec.
Saunders, Thomas & Polley Morris, 19 Dec. 1803, Edward Morris sec.
    Note from John Saunders, father of Thomas, wit: Bolling
    Wright - Note from Jesse Morris, father of Polley - wit:
    John Feagins.

Savage, John & Mary Taylor, 1 May 1787, James Day sec.

Scott, Arcey & Elizabeth Chavis, 9 Jan. 1809, Fred Ivey sec. Note
    from Elizabeth Chavis, mother of Elizabeth.
Scott, Robert & Elizabeth Pettus, 8 Sept. 1806, William Pettus sec.
    Note from Samuel Pettus, Sr.
Scott, Samuel, of Dinwiddie Co. & Martha Henly, 5 Jan. 1792, Wm.
    Johnson, Gent. sec.

Selden, Joseph & Mary Burwell, 11 Apr. 1785, Samuel Goode sec.

Seward, Isaac & Lucy Valentine, 25 Oct. 1803, Isham Valentine sec.
Seward, John & Betsey Malone, 2 June, 1771, Drury Malone sec.
Seward, John, Jr. & Sarah Hanserd, 6 Dec. 1799, Richard Hanserd sec.

Sharp, M. Turner & Martha Jones, 24 Jan. 1797, James Elam sec. Note
from Richard Jones, father of Martha, ack. before Abraham Koen.
Sharp, Turner & Elizabeth Jones, dau. Richard, 11 May 1807 - Note
from Charles Jones, G'dn. of Elizabeth - wit: Samuel Williams
& Aaron Haskins.

Shaw, John & Patsey Crowder, 10 Nov. 1800, Thos. Merriott sec.
Shaw, John & Susanna Cortis, 4 Aug. 1790, Drury Creadle sec.

Shackleford, Zachariah & Susannah Allgood, 9 Oct. 1797, John Allgood
sec.

Shearer, James & Nancy Allen, 13 Nov. 1797, John Cox sec.

Shell, Freeman & Beckey Tisdale, 18 Mar. 1806, Bartlett Cox sec.
Shell, Herman, of Brunswick Co. & Martha Epps, 9 Oct. 1790, John
Epps sec.
Shell, John & Lizzy Malone, 28 May 1786, Hardy Jones sec.

Short, Batte & Patsey Lett, 30 May 1791, James Bing sec.
Short, Batty & Seller Murdock, 2 Nov. 1798, John Carrol sec.
Short, Edmund & Susanna Bilbo, 6 Apr. 1787, John Bilbo sec.
Short, Freeman & Elizabeth Evans, 1 Sept. 1808, Geo. Finch sec.
Short, Isaac & Susanna Toone, 12 Jan. 1795, John Steagall sec.
Short, Jacob & Phebe Finch, 23 Oct. 1794, Wm. Finch sec.
Short, John & Rebecca Goode, 28 Jan. 1807, Edward Holloway sec.
Short, Wyatt & Mary Adams, 11 Dec. 1809, Richard M. Allen sec.

Sims, Charles & Lucy Hutcheson, 21 Jan. 1794, Charles Hutcheson
sec.
Sims, Leonard & Sarah Swepson, 12 Mar. 1770, Richard Swepson sec.

Simmons, James & Morning Lark, 3 Jan. 1805, James Noel sec.
Simmons, John & Elizabeth Baugh, 23 Sept. 1790, James Baugh sec.
Simmons, Joseph & Elizabeth Harrison, 8 May 1797, Sam. Simmons
sec. Note from John & Sarah Ogburn, G'dns. of Elizabeth - wit: Benj. S. Harrison.
Simmons, Samuel & Elizabeth Coleman, 7 Aug. 1795, Thomas Coleman sec.

Simpson, Edwin & Mahala Stewart, 12 Dec. 1808, Saunders Harris sec.

Singleton, John & Ann Daly, 4 Sept. 1793, Daniel Daly sec.
Singleton, John & Rebecca Crook, 8 Oct. 1801, James Nash sec.
Singleton, Robert & Polley Thompson, 30 Dec. 1795, William Barritt
sec.
Singleton, William & Susanna Gwaltney, 13 Jan. 1798, Richard Stone
sec.

Skelton, Edward & Phebee Walker, 22 Dec. 1803, Bartley Cheatham
sec.
Skelton, Thomas & Martha Watson, 29 Dec. 1799, Jordan Bennett sec.

Smith, Anderson & Elizabeth Maryann Avary, 9 June 1783, John Avary sec.
Smith, Archer & Mary Brame, 11 Apr. 1796, James Norment sec.
Smith, Augustin, Jr. & Nancy Rudd, 8 Feb. 1790, William Insco sec.
Smith, Benjamin & Caty Page, 2 Apr. 1803, Thomas Smith sec.
Smith, Daniel & Patsey Poindexter, 10 Dec. 1792, Robert Smith sec.
Smith, Ichabob & Lucy Pennington, 31 Oct. 1795, Henry Pennington sec.
Smith, James & Elinor Hyde, 12 Dec. 1791, Robert Hyde sec.
Smith, John Prior & Susanna Smith, dau. Drury, 7 Oct. 1776, Achilles
        Jeffries sec.
Smith, John & Nancy Smith, 29 Mar. 1791, Augustin Smith sec.
Smith, John & Sally Ellis, 29 Jan. 1796, John Loyd sec.
Smith, John P. & Polley Oslin, 30 Oct. 1801, Isaac Oslin sec.
Smith, Joseph & Elizabeth Burnett, 11 Sept. 1792, Silvanus Ingram sec.
Smith, Joshua & Oliver Brown, 6 Jan. 1801, William Hutcheson sec.
Smith, Matthew & Sibbe Lambert, 24 Nov. 1787, Joseph Lambert sec.
Smith, Obadiah & Tabitha Wilson, 22 May 1798, Jos. Wilson sec.
Smith, Robert & Nancy Norment, 8 Jan. 1787, Thos. Norment sec.
Smith, Samuel Hancock & Jane Wright Russell, 24 July 1806, Thos.
        A. Jones sec.
Smith, Sherod & Faithy Holmes, 21 Dec. 1786, William Starling sec.
Smith, Thomas & Mary Wilson, 28 Sept. 1795, James Day sec.
Smith, Thomas & Patsey Hubbard, 15 Mar. 1806, John Hubbard sec.
Smith, William & Anne Pitts, 13 Oct. 1787, William Norvell sec.
Smith, William H. & Mary Walker, 22 Feb. 1808, Matthew Walker sec.

Smithson, Bartley & Sarah Weatherford, 30 Nov. 1799, Freeman
        Weatherford sec. Note from William Weatherford, father of
        Sarah.
Smithson, Briant & Dolley Burton, 13 June 1796, Peter Puryear sec.
Smithson, Charles & Betsey Cheatham, 8 Dec. 1800, Saml. Cheatham sec.

Somervill, George C. & Elenor H. Birchett, 23 Mar. 1811, Henry
        Hicks sec.

Sparks, William & Judith Thompson, 9 Jan. 1804, Bernard Thompson
        sec.

Spain, Abraham & Elizabeth Allen, 6 May 1795, Henderson Wade sec.
Spain, Daniel & Judith Allen, 18 Nov. 1802, Abraham Spain sec.
Spain, Thomas & Elizabeth Hasking, 6 Jan. 1797, William Lucas sec.
Spain, Thomas & Nancy Stewart, 14 Sept. 1801, Frederick Ivy sec.
Spain, William & Judith Harris, 13 Dec. 1802, James Clack sec.

Speaks, George & Martha Matthews, 8 Nov. 1809, John Matthews sec.

Speed, John & Polly Wade, 3 July 1798, Joseph Speed, Jr. sec. Note
        from Joseph Townes, G'dn. of Polly.
Speed, John James & Lucy Swepson, 26 Jan. 1801, C.H.Baskervill sec.
Speed, Robert & Polley A. Coleman, 25 Jan. 1809, William Coleman
        sec.

Spurlock, William & Tempy Nanny, 9 Dec. 1798, Wm.Roberts sec.
Spurlock, Zachariah & Betsey Mealer, 13 Oct. 1792, John Farrar sec.

State, Richard, of Brunswick Co. & Elizabeth Vaughan, 12 Nov. 1802,
John Saunders sec.

Stainback, Robert, of Brunswick Co. & Polley Andrews, 13 Dec. 1804,
Isaac Arnold sec.

Stegall, George & Mary T. Short, 23 Jan. 1799, Henry Finch sec.

Stewart (Stuart-Steward), Archer & Jincy Chavos, 14 Aug. 1809, Edward
Brandon sec.
Stewart, Bartlett & Elizabeth Drew, 21 Oct. 1807, George Guy sec.
Stewart, Charles & Salra Elam, 14 Mar. 1808, Fredk. Ivey sec.
Stewart, George & Jean Chandler, 27 Dec. 1797, Moses Stewart sec.
Note - "I hereby certify that I have sold George (commonly
of late called George Stewart) to Moses Stewart and
therefore I have no claim or title in him whatspever.
Given under my hand and seal this 25 day of December,
1797 - Zacharias Mallet" Wit: Wm. Jones & Howel Mallet.
Stewart, James, Jr. & Ryte Chavous, 11 Feb. 1788, James Stewart,
Sr. sec.
Stewart, John Ginnet & Polley Manning, 9 Dec. 1794, Earbe Chavous
sec. Note from Susanna Chavous, mother of Polley.
Stewart, Matthew & Siller Walden, 25 Feb. 1799, William Chandler
sec.
Stewart, Matt & Eliza Stewart, 8 Feb. 1802, Miles Dunston sec.
Stewart, Thomas & Sary Cattiler, 15 July 1800, Richerson Farrar
sec.

Steagall, John & Susanna Bedingefield, 12 Dec. 1786, William
Finch sec.

Stembridge, James & Elizabeth Gregory, 31 Dec. 1801, John Stembridge sec.
Stembridge, John & Salley Graves, 24 Dec. 1802, Obadiah Belcher
sec.

Stolcop, Tobias & Lucy Pearce, 9 Jan. 1809, Balaam Ezell sec.

Stone, Asher & Frankey Cox, 13 Nov. 1797, John Cox sec.
Stone, Drury & Nancy Hunley, 12 Nov. 1798, Wm. Hunley sec.
Stone, Elijah & Rebecca Roberts, 13 Aug. 1792, Thomas Roberts
sec.
Stone, James & Johanna Jones, 10 Jan. 1791, Daniel Jones sec.
Stone, James & Elizabeth Griffin, 12 Mar. 1810, Elijah Griffin
sec.
Stone, John & Elizabeth Hutcheson, 11 Dec. 1797, Wm. Stone sec.
Stone, Jordan & Margaret Griffin, 17 Dec. 1803, Elijah Griffin
sec.
Stone, William, Jr. & Susanna Hutcheson, 21 Nov. 1795, Jesse
Corsbley sec. Note from William Stone, G'dn. of
Susanna ¬ wit. John Stone.

Stroud, Willis & Elizabeth Blanton, 11 Sept. 1792, George
Small sec.

Stuart (Stuard-Stewart), James & Precilla Stuart, 14 Nov. 1791, John
   Walden sec.
Stuart, Moses & Polley Walden, 20 Dec. 1788, Eaton Walden sec. Note
   from John Cha. Walden, father of Polley.
Stuard, William, of Brunswick Co. & Hissey Corn, 21 ____ , Robt. Corn
   sec.

Sturdivant, Randol & Disa Rainey, 27 May 1776, Francis Rainey sec.
Sturdivant, Randolph & Mourning Lambert, 5 Jan. 1797, David Thomas
   sec.   Note from Joseph Lambert, father of Disa.

Swepson, Richard & (Mrs) Mary Tabb, 12 Apr. 1779, Achilles Jeffries
   sec.
Swepson, William M. & Elizabeth I. Speed, 27 Mar. 1805, John James
   Speed sdc.

Tabb, Edward L. & Elizabeth Blair Burwell, 31 Jan. 1791, G. H.
   Baskervill sec.   Note from Lewis Burwell, father of Elizabeth.

Talley, George & Lucy McDaniel, 12 Dec. 1787, James Moore sec.
   Note from John & Marey McDaniel, parents of Lucy.
Talley, Grief & Lucy Curtis, 16 Sept. 1799, Drury Creedle sec.
Talley, Larkin & Polly Blacketer, 27 Sept. 1805, Sam'l. Bugg sec.
Talley, Russell & Elizabeth Creedle, 14 July 1791, Bryant Creedle
   sec.

Tanner, David & Martha Ferrell, 6 May 1802, Hutchins Ferrell sec.
Tanner, Jonathan & Mary Young, 5 June 1798, Allen Young sec.
Tanner, Ludwell & Lucy Holmes, 2 Dec. 1781, John Baskervill sec.
Tanner, Richard & Nancy Andrews, 15 Oct. 1808, Varney Andrews sec.

Tarry, George & Sarah Taylor, 7 Dec. 1790, Anderson Taylor sec.
Tarry, Robert & Nancy Smith, 10 June, 1793, Joseph Townes sec.
Tarry, Samuel & Amey Pettus, 8 July 1799, Wm. Coleman sec.
Tarry, Samuel & Mary Brown, 14 Mar. 1808, Geo. Craighead sec.

Taylor, Absolom & Martha C. Parrett, 29 Dec. 1809, John Hudgin sec.
Taylor, Clark & Elizabeth Whitehead, 13 Feb. 1786, Richd. Swepson
   sec.
Taylor, David & Rebecca Dortch, 9 May 1778, Wm. Taylor sec.
Taylor, Goodwyn & Nancy Drumright, 10 Jan. 1794, William Drumright
   sec.
Taylor, Goodwyn & Elizabeth Davis, 5 May 1802, David Dortch sec.
Taylor, Howell & Susannah Young, 30 Dec. 1778, Samuel Young sec.
Taylor, James & Prycillah Fox, 9 Dec. 1801, Josiah Floyd sec.
Taylor, Jesse & Phebe Moody, 27 June 1789, Francis Moody sec.
   Note from Henry Moody, father of Phebe.
Taylor (Speeds) William & Molley Gober, 4 July 1798, John Gober
   sec.
Taylor, John & Happy Cook, 5 Jan. 1802, Abel Dortch sec.
Taylor, Jones & Joice Lark, 11 Apr. 1780, John Holmes sec.
Taylor, Joseph & Elizabeth Willis, 29 Feb. 1796, Francis Jones
   sec.   Note from Swepson Jeffries, G'dn. of Elizabeth.

Taylor, Richard B. & Mary C. Gregory, 4 Dec. 1798, Richard Gregory
sec.
Taylor, Thomas & Salley Benford, 28 Sept. 1792, Wm. Drumright sec.
Taylor, Thomas & Lucy Crutchfield, 24 Jan. 1797, Wm. Drumright sec.
Taylor, Thomas & Salley Lark, 26 Dec. 1797, Samuel Lark sec.
Taylor, Thomas & Martha Cocke Hamblin, 18 Oct. 1800, Reuben Vaughan
sec. Note from Agness Hamblin, mother of Martha - wit:
Littleberry Battes & Henry Taylor.
Taylor, Thomas & Martha Leach, 5 Aug. 1808, Francis Gregory sec.
Note from bride signed "Patsey Leach".
Taylor, William & Elizabeth Holloway, 26 Apr. 1785, Samuel Durham sec.
Taylor, William Ladd & Mary Ambrose, 2 Dec. 1785, William Drumright
sec.

Temple, Samuel & Susanna Coppedge, 11 Nov. 1793, Chas. Coppedge sec.

Terry, Roaling & Mary Wadkins, 12 Oct. 1807, Overton Wiles sec.

Thomas, Bennett & Putres Jones, 21 Mar. 1810, William Jones sec.
Thomas, Billey & Lucy Stuart, 10 Apr. 1786, Francis Short sec.
Thomas, William & Frances Carless, 20 Dec. 1790, Peter Thomas, Jr.
sec.

Thompson, Bernard & Milley Yates, 10 Dec. 1804, John Walton sec.
Thompson, Charles & Frances Daly, 9 Dec. 1782, Phil Ricks sec.
Thompson, James Mines & Nancy Jackson, 3 Jan. 1789, John Allen sec.
Note from John Thompson.
Thompson, James & Susanna Nunnery, 27 Aug. 1806, Daniel Tucker, Sr.
sec.
Thompson, John & Sarah Thompson, 8 May 1775, Asa Oliver sec.
Thompson, John & Phebe Tisdale, 12 Jan. 1795, William Thompson sec.
Thompson, John & Nancy Burnett, 13 Apr. 1801, Richard Burnett sec.
Thompson, John & Mary Sally, 12 Oct. 1807, Ste. P. Pool sec.
Thompson, Richard & Frances Anne Watts, 14 June, 1802, Hy. Ashton
sec. Note from Anna Watts, mother of Frances.
Thompson, William & Nancy H. Butler, 27 Dec. 1802, James Thompson
sec.
Thompson, William & Mary Hailestock, 19 Feb. 1808, Abel Stewart
sec.

Thomson, William, Jr. & Patsy Laffoon, 7 Feb. 1805, William Thomson, Sr. sec.

Thomerson, Banister & Mary Singleton, 25 July 1795, William Thomerson sec.
Thomerson, James & Molley Thompson, 4 Dec. 1804, David Hicks sec.

Threadgill, Thomas & Tabitha Ingram, 9 Sept. 1782, Reuben Vaughan
sec.

Tillotson, Edward & Milley Gold, 2 Feb. 1808, John Hailey sec.
Notes from William Tillotson, father of Edward, & Thomas
Hailey, father of Milley

Tillotson, John & Delphia Yancey, 16 Jan. 1801, Richard Murray sec.

Tisdale, John & Nancy Clark, 13 Mar. 1787, Thomas Clark sec.

Toone (Toon), Argelon & Mary Freeman, 13 Oct. 1783, James Hix sec.
Toone, James & Milley Daniel, 9 Apr. 1770, Will Taylor sec. Note
    from William Daniel, father of Milley.
Toone, Lewis & Rebecah Moore, 15 Aug. 1787, Francis Lewis sec.
Toon, Lewis & Millicence Richards, 11 Feb. 1805, Abraham Keen sec.
    Note from W. Richards, father of Millicence.
Toone, Tavener & Ann Marshall, 20 May 1809, George Bilbo sec.
Toone, Thomas & Winney Garner, 11 Aug. 1800, Richard Brown sec.
    Note from James Garner, father of Winney.
Toone, William & Elizabeth Hamblin,22 Mar. 1786, Isaac Pulley sec.
Townes, Henry & Polley Davis, 31 Dec. 1784, William Townes sec.
    Note from Barton Davis, father of Polley.
Townes, Joseph & Isabella Wade, 28 June, 1784, Henry Townes, of.
    Halifax Co. sec.

Townsen, Peter & Lucy Hundley, 11 July 1808, William Hunley sec.

Traylor, Cary & Elizabeth Thompson, 7 Nov. 1786, John Johnson sec.

Trice, Thomas & Mary Green, 11 Aug. 1777, Edmond Taylor, Gent. sec.

Tucker, Daniel & Jincey Cardin, 17 July 1787, George Stainback sec.
    Note from John Cardin, father of Jincey - wit. Robert Cardin.
Tucker, Daniel, Jr. & Mary Parrish, 8 Feb. 1808, William Parrish
    sec.
Tucker, George & Eddy Short, 23 Apr. 1800, Daniel Tucker sec.
Tucker, Harwood & Nancy Mason, 9 Jan. 1809, William Stone sec.
Tucker, Isham & Roase Eaton, 2 Feb. 1786, James Bing sec.
Tucker, Isham & Sarah Booker, 11 May 1803, William Rew sec.
Tucker, James & Catherine Tucker, 14 Dec. 1772, Ro. Williams sec.
Tucker, James & Jane Tucker, 6 Sept. 1809, William Insco sec.
Tucker, James & Ruth Puckett, 17 May 1810, G. B. Hudson sec.
Tucker, Jesse & Nancy Carroll, 7 Nov. 1793, John Carroll sec.
Tucker, John & Salley Nunnery, 22 Jan. 1793, Chevnal Dearden sec.
Tucker, John & Francis Tucker, 10 Dec. 1798, Leonard Keeton sec.
Tucker, Littleberry & Elizabeth Kelley, 22 Dec. 1797, John
    Tucker sec.
Tucker, Robert & Sarah Smith, 12 Nov. 1787, Edwd. Elam sec.
Tucker, Tapla &oNancy Kelley, 9 Dec. 1799, Danl. Tucker sec.
Tucker, Worsham & Mary Gordan, 5 Dec. 1804, John Gosee sec.

Tuder, John & Milley Spurlock, 16 July 1786, Zachariah Spurlock
    sec.

Turner, Bailey & Susanna Easter, 1 Dec. 1792, John Oliver sec.
Turner, Drury & Tallathacuma Jackson, 11 Dec. 1802, Matthew
    Jackson sec.
Turner, John & Mary Hutcheson, 13 Oct. 1800, Arcolius Walker sec.
Turner, John & Rebeccah Taylor, 8 Dec. 1800, James Taylor, Jr.
    sec.

Turner, Stephen & Martha Weight, 11 Mar. 1801, Aysten Weight sec.
Turner, Terisha & Joanah Reaves, 19 Dec. 1785, John Burton sec.
    Notes from Stepehen Turner & Thomas Rives.
Turner, Thomas Weaver & Betty Merrymoon, 1 Nov. 1786, Isham Merry-
    moon sec. Note from James Turner, father of Thomas.

Vaughan, Balaam & Polly Burnes, 11 Dec. 1809, Robert Burnes sec.
Vaughan, Binnes & Martha L. Arnold, 20 June, 1798, Thomas Edmonson
    sec.
Vaughan, David & Patty Kirks, 3 Aug. 1803, John Hudgins sec.
Vaughan, David & Philadelphia Griffin1 14 Dec. 1807, Hezekiah
    Yancey sec. Note from James Griffin, father of Phila-
    delphia.
Vaughan, Edmond H. & Sally H. Walker, 5 June 1809, F. E. Walker sec.
Vaughan, Henry G. & Nancy O. Wade, 3 Jan. 1803, William Wade sec.
Vaughan, Ingram & Ann Lewis, 20 Aug. 1785, W. Baskervill sec.
    Note from Edward Lewis, G'dn. of Ann.
Vaughan, Ishmael & Caty Roberts, 24 Oct. 1787, William Roberts sec.
Vaughan, Jairus & Hannah Vaughan, 11 July 1796, Craddock Vaughan
    sec. Note from R. Vaughan, father of Hannah.
Vaughan, James & Susannah Harriss, 11 June, 1802, Richard Jeff-
    ries sec. Note from William Harris, father of Susannah.
Vaughan, James & Mary Crow, 26 Dec. 1808, William Crow sec.
Vaughan, John & Nancy Hayes, 13 Dec. 1802, Starky Hayes sec.
Vaughan, Robert C. & Rebecca M. Davis, 4 Jan. 1806, Bushrod Webb
    sec. Notes from Ambrose Vaughan, father of Robert & from
    Randolph Davis, father of Rebecca.
Vaughan, Thomas & Ann Smith, 12 Oct. 1772, Swepson Jeffries sec.
Vaughan, Thomas & Martha Lewis, 8 Oct. 1781, Edward Lewis sec.
Vaughan, Thomas & Mary Alford Blackbourn, 11 Mar. 1799, John
    Wilson sec.
Vaughan, William & Elizabeth Saunders __ Mar. 1794, Ambrose
    Vaughan sec. Notes from Richard Vaughan, father of
    William & from John Saunders, father of Elizabeth.
Vaughan, William & Anne C. Gregory, 6 Apr. 1795, Richard Gregory
    sec.
Vaughan, James & Judy Spain, 11 Dec. 1797, Sterling Spain sec.
    Note from Thomas Spain, father of Judy.
Vaughan, Woody & Sarah Farrar, 11 Dec. 1804, Sanford Bowers sec.
    Note from George Farrar, father of Sarah - wit. Hilsmons
    Farrar.

Venable, Samuel, of Prince Edward Co. & Amy Anderson, 5 Mar.
    1782 - Thomas Anderson sec.

Valentine (Volontine) Buckner & Sine Chavous, 21 Dec. 1802,
    Boling Chavous sec.
Volontine, Charles & Nancy Chavous, 28 Nov. 1785, Thomas Macklin
    sec.
Valentine, John & Mary McLin, 4 Jan. 1797, Earby Chavous sec.

Wade, William & Martha Russell, 9 Nov. 1767, William Robertson &
John Russell sec.
Wade, William & Polley Mealer, 12 Aug. 179 __ , Willis Vaughan sec.
Wade, Henderson & Elizabeth Wilburn, 6 Jan. 1795, William Harrison
sec.

Wagstaff, Allen & Susannah Overton, 12 Dec. 1803, Philemon Hurt, Jr.
sec.
Wagstaff, Bazzell & Elizabeth Camp, 5 Mar. 1806, Allen Wagstaff sec.
Wagstaff, Britain & Anne Freeman, dau. Allen, 7 Feb. 1778, Allen
Freeman sec.

Walden, Eaton & Nanney Evans, 20 Dec. 1788, Moses Stuart sec. Note
from Charles Evans, father of Nanney.
Walden, Jarrel & Mourning Jackson, 16 Sept. 1801, John Harris sec.
Walden, Jesse & Milley Stewart, 6 Apr. 1805, Fredk. Ivy sec.
Walden, John & Betsey Stewart, 21 Apr. 1804, Kinchin Chavos sec.

Walton, John & Dolley Ricks, 14 Oct. 1798, Richd. Brown sec.

Walker, Arealius & Nancy Turner, 23 Nov. 1784, William Allen sec.
Walker, Daniel, of Nottoway Co. & Mary Brown, 5 Aug. 1793, Thomas
Brown sec.
Walker, Freeman & Polley Toone, 12 July 1789, Lewis Toone sec.
Walker, George & Phebe Cheatham, 14 Dec. 1789, Obadiah Cheatham
sec. Note from Daniel Cheatham, father of Phebe.
Walker, John & Anna Gregory, 12 Nov. 1798, Thomas Reamy sec.
Walker, Joseph R. & Dolley Winfield, 6 Dec. 1796, William Abernathy
sec. Note from Joshua Winfield, father of Dolley - wit. A⁻ :
Aurther FreemanWinfield.
Walker, Matthew & Rebecca Powers, 21 Dec. 1805, Jno. Turner,Jr. sec.
Walker, Matthew & Salley Stone, 4 Oct. 1809, William Stone sec.
Walker, Richard H. & Nancy Vaughan, 10 July 1798, Thomas Vaughan
sec.
Walker, William & Mary Bugg, 7 Aug. 1779, Henry Pennington sec.
Note from John & Lucy Bugg.

Wall, Benjamin & Mary S. Bugg, 2 Apr. 1800, Fredk. Wall sec.
Note from Molley Bugg, mother of Mary - wit. Mary Sardefer
Bugg & Jesse Bugg.
Wall, Burwell & Mary Burks, 30 Sept. 1794, Miles House sec. Note
from Mary stating that she is 25 years old. wit. John
Dupree & Freeman Short.
Wall, David S. & Rebecca J. Short, 3 July 1805, George Stegall
sec.
Wall, Frederick & Patsey Wooton Daniel, 13 June 1803, William
Daniel sec.
Wall, Henry & Salley Daniel, 17 Dec. 1810, Frederick Wall sec.
Wall, John, of Halifax Co. & Amey Hall, 10 Dec. 1787, James
Hall sec,
Wall, John, of Halifax Co. & Meloda Overby, 22 Feb. 1808, Peter
Overby, Jr. sec.
Wall, Major & Mary James, 10 Jan. 1803, Frederick Porch sec.
Wall, Thomas & Eliz. H. Short, 30 Sept. 1797, Freeman Short sec.

Wall, Thomas & Jane Edmundson, 13 Jan. 1800, John Whobry sec.

Wallace, David & Nancy Mills, 22 Mar. 1798, Larkin Crowder sec.

Waller, Daniel & Frances Holmes, 29 Apr. 1788, John Waller sec.
Waller, James & Susanna Wilson, 16 Mar. 1792, James Wilson sec.
Waller, John & Ann Holmes, 5 Mar. 1782, John Ballard sec.
Waller, Starling & Rebecca Drumright, 1 Sept. 1796, William Drum-
    right sec.

Warren, John &Betsey Holmes, 5 Dec. 1792, Walter Leigh sec.
Warren, Merriott & Mary Holmes, 17 Dec. 1794, Benjamin Suggett sec.
    Note from Samuel Holmes, Sr. father of Mary.
Warren, William & Lucinda Holmes, 17 Apr. 1798, Samuel Holmes sec.

Watts, Richard & Lucy Collier, 10 Mar. 1806, William Lipford sec.

Watkins, James & Ann Nuckolls, 9 Sept. 1789, Philip Morgan sec.
Watkins, Thomas & Elliner Farrar, 8 Nov. 1790, Thomas Farrar sec.

Watson, James & Polley Taylor, 27 Jan. 1796, Abel Dortch sec.
Watson, James T. & Elizabeth Lark, 6 Oct. 1803, Saml. Lark, Sr.
    sec.
Watson, Thomas & Susanna Taylor, 27 Dec. 1791, William Poole sec.
    Note from Abel Dortch.

Weatherford, Freeman & Polley Smith, 8 Dec. 1800, Richd. Thompson
    sec. Note from Buckner Smith, father of Polley.

Webb, Abdias &Patty Tain, 15 Dec. 1790, Fredk. Raney sec.
Webb, Bushrod & Catherine Lavingston, 7 Jan. 1800, Mark L. Jackson
    sec.
Webb, John & Nancy Winn, 13 Sept. 1802, Littleberry Winn sec.
Webb, John & Sine Blankenship, 16 Dec. 1802, Mark Lambert Jackson
    sec.

Webster, Samuel & Charlotte Winkler, 1 Aug. 1788, Richardson Davis
    sec.

Wells, Baker & Levina Underwood, 10 Sept. 1798, Zacheus Ezell sec.
Wells, David & Nancy Garrett, 11 Oct. 1799, Elijah Wells sec.
    Note from Thomas Garrott, father of Nancy.
Wells, Elijah & Sarah Ferrell, 14 Sept. 1795, John Hudson sec.

Westbrook, Jesse & Amy Weatherford, 9 Dec. 1805, James Baker sec.
Westbrook, Randolph & Happy Salley, 10 Dec. 1798, John Allgood
    sec.
Westbrook, Thomas & Salley B_____, 9 Dec. 1805, Jesse West-
    brook sec.

Westmoreland, Robert & Polly Pennington, 5 Dec. 1804, George
    Tucker sec.

Whitworth, Samuel & Mary H. Walden, 9 Mar. 1778, Peter Burton sec.

Whitlow, James &Penelope Haywood, 18 May 1803, John Bilbo sec.
Whitlow, William, Jr. & Mary Sanders, 12 Oct. 1795, Charles Burton sec.

White, Henry & Rebecca Davis, 21 Dec. 1805, Robert Davis sec.
White, James & Mary Greenwood, 22 Feb. 1786, William Willis sec.
    Note from Thomas Greenwood.
White, John & Nancy Baker, 12 Mar. 1787, Thomas Feild sec.
White, John & Nancy Holloway, 12 Dec. 1797, Edward Holloway sec.
White, Larken &*Nelley Dedman, 9 Dec. 1793, Henry Dedman sec.
White, Robert &|Jane Winn, 5 Dec. 1807, John Dedman sec.
White, William & Frances Greenwood, 21 June 1791, John Greensood
    sec.   Note from Thomas Greenwood.

Whobry, John & Sarah Bugg, 6 Mar. 1794, John Bugg sec.

Wilson, Archibald & Martha Bevill, 26 Oct. 1785, Hutchins Burton
    sec.
Wilson, Caleb, of Orange CO., N. C. & Elizabeth Ballard, 5 Jan.
    1803, Francis Ballard sec.
Wilson, Daniel & Elizabeth Cheatham, dau. Leonard Cheatham,
    28 Aug. 1778, William Waddill sec.
Wilson, Henry & Caty Waller, 25 June, 1790, Daniel Walker sec.
Wilson, John & Elizabeth Smith, 12 Sept. 1791, Thomas Burnett
    sec.
Wilson, John & Nancy Goodram, 2 Jan. 1793, Robert Baskervill sec.
Wilson, Miles & Margaret Feild, 13 Feb. 1809, Erasmous Kennon
    sec.   Note from Jane Feild, mother of Margaret.
Wilson, Robert & Eleanor Dedman, 9 June 1794, Larkin White sec.
Wilson, Robert & Hannah Stone, 9 May 1808, William Stone sec.
Wilson, Thomas & Elizabeth Vaughan, 13 Nov. 1789, Robert Bur-
    chett sec.
Wilson, William & Rebecca Brown, 9 Sept. 1782, Thomas Brown sec.

Wilburn, Julius & Lucy Puryear, 15 Mar. 1798, William Vowell
    sec. Note from Thomas Puryear, father of Lucy.
Wilborn, Thomas & Phebe Moore, 11 July 1800, William Jones sec.
    Note from Geo. Moore, father of Phebe.
Wilburn, William & Patty Avery, 28 Feb. 1782, James Harrison sec.
Wilburn, William & Elizabeth Hudson, 28 Jan. 1793, William
    Hudson sec.

Wiles, Martin & Claresy Epperson, 13 Sept. 1802, Jos. Epperson
    sec.

Wilkins, Charles, of Rutherford Co., N. C. & Elizabeth Puryear,
    22 June 1795, John Farrar sec.

Wills, Robert & Jane Colley, 12 Oct. 1788, Edward Colley sec.

Willis, Edward & Polley Moore, 21 Dec. 1801, James Browder sec.
Willis, James & Lucy Nash, 14 Nov. 1783, John Crews sec.
Willis, John & Salley Pulliam, 10 Dec. 1792. Richd. Carter sec.
Willis, William & Lucy Moore, 16 Apr. 1782, James Willis sec.

Williams, David & Milley Newton, 11 June 1804, John Williams sec.
Williams, James & Mary Durham, 8 May 1797, Rusebius Stone sec.
Williams, John & Elizabeth Taylor, 26 Oct. 1791, Samuel Holmes, Jr.
    sec.
Williams, Jeremiah & Dolly Carter, 27 Nov. 1802, Jos. N. Meredith sec.
Williams, Leroy & Amey Mills, 24 Dec. 1794, George Baker sec.
    Note from Susanna Stubbs, mother of Amey.
Williams, Thomas & Sally Alderson, 27 July 1808, Robert Garrott sec.
Williams, William & Judith Baker, 8 Jan. 1796, Geo. Baker sec.

Williamson, John & Susanna Yancey, 3 Sept. 1802, Richard Murry sec.
    Note from Robert Yancey, father of Susanna.
Williamson, Merryman & Sally Thomerson, 29 July 1803, Archibald
    Merryman sec.
Williamson, Robert & Mary Yancey, 25 Jan. 1793, W. Baskervill sec.

Winn, Banister & Nancy Naish, 11 Dec. 1809, Benj. Blake sec.
Winn, Harrison & Frances Haile, 11 July 1785, Tho: Haile sec.
Winn, Littleberry & Mary Maynard, 29 Dec. 1783, William Maynard sec.
Winn, Richard & Sarah Hall, 14 Aug. 1775, James Hall sec.

Winfield, Arthur Freeman & Susannah Courtney, 2 June 1786, Saml.
    Holmes sec.
Winfield, Joel & Polley Booth, 3 Mar. 1801, Joshua Winfield sec.

Wootton, John & Mary Christopher, 18 Mar. 1785, William Daniel sec.
Wootton, Samuel & Martha Hyde, 10 Nov. 1788, John Hyde sec.

Woodson, Miller, Jr. & Sophia W. Hendrick, 8 Aug. 1803, Amasa
    Palmer sec.
Woodson, Tscharner & Lucy Michaux, 8 Sept. 1788, Wm. Hendrick sec.
    Note from Jos. Michaus, G'dn. of Lucy.

Wortman, Henry & Tabitha Eppes, 24 Nov. 1787, Isham Eppes sec.

Wortham, James & Jincy McQuie, 11 Nov. 1799, Thomas A. Jones sec.

Worsham, John & Lucy Hamblin, 12 Nov. 1804, Ste. Pettepool sec.
Worsham, Ste. & Nancy Blanks, 14 Sept. 1807, Daniel Jones sec.

Wright, Austin, Sr. & Lucy Holloway, 1 Mar. 1806, Francis Ballard
    sec.
Wright, Anderson & Phebe Malone, 27 May 1793, William Poole,Jr.
    sec.
Wright, Anderson & Elizabeth Langford, 6 Dec. 1794, James Watson
    sec.
Wright, Bolling & Milly Saunders, 30 July 1787, John Feagins sec.
    Note from John Saunders, father of Milly.
Wright, Claiborne & Patsey Nanney, 27 Dec. 1792, Highburry
    Nanney sec.
Wright, David, of Lunenburg Co. & Nancy Wright, 28 Dec. 1797,
    Roderick Wright sec.
Wright, James & Sarah Easter, 23 Dec. 1784, Leonard Smith sec.
Wright, John & Sarah Fox, 3 Oct. 1797, William Taylor (Speeds)
    sec. Note from Richard Fox, father of Sarah.

Wright, John (of. Austin) & Salley Holmes, 13 May 1801, John Holmes sec.
Wright, John & Rebecca Oslin, 19 June 1802, Isaac Oslin sec.
Wright, Robert, of Brunswick Co. & Nancy Wright, 16 Nov. 1792,
    Austin Wright sec.
Wright, Roderick & Martha Cleaton, 19 Sept. 1795, Thomas Cleaton, Jr..
    sec.
Wright, Sterling & Silviah Davis, 4 July 1788, Josiah Floyd sec.
Wright, William & Nancy Palmer, 12 Dec. 1804, Thomas Wright sec.

Wyatt, Walter & Elizabeth Brame, 16 Dec. 1793, James Brame sec.

Yancey, Hezekiah & Salley Worsham, 10 Oct. 1808, John Williamson
    sec.
Yancey, John & Mary Hamblin, 14 Oct. 1799, Daniel Jones sec.
    Note from Thomas Hamblin, father of Mary.
Tancey, Minge & Frankey Knott, 9 May 1808, Samuel C. Brame sec.
Yancey, Robert & Agness Wilkerson, 11 Oct. 1796, Francis Griffin
    sec.

Yates, Edwd. Randolph, of Amelia Co., & Elizabeth Murray, dau.
    John, 20 Sept. 1783, Asa Oliver sec.   Note from William
    Yates, G'dn. of Eded. Randolph.

Young, Allen & Sarah Davis, 22 May 1779, Samuel Young sec.
Young, Coleman & Mary Standley, 18 Dec. 1788, James Standley sec.
Young, John & Jane Swepson, 24 Jan. 1784, Enos Easter sec.
Young, Juhonias & Rebeccah Royster, 15 Dec. 1788, George Royster
    sec.

Abernathy, Lucy 14; Martha 41

Adams, Lucy 1,19; Lizey 12; Mary
    46; Rebecca 14

Akins, Jelley 45

Alderson, Sally 56

Alexander, Martha 40

Allgood (Algood) Betsey H. 34;
    Dicy 27; Elizabeth 5,10,11;
    Judith 23; Lucy 12; Nancy 30;
    Sarah 27; Susannah 46

Allen, Anne 3; Elizabeth 26,34,47;
    Judith 47; Leanner 43;
    Margaret 34; Nancy 46;
    Rebecca 2; Sally 1; Susanna
    42

Alvis, Betsey 10

Ambrose, Mary 50

Andrews, Anne 2,7; Elizabeth 19;
    Nancy 49; Patsey 19; Polley
    48

Anderson, Amy 52; Lucy 21; Mary
    32; Sarah 30; Susannah 32

Apperson, Lucy 44; Martha 18;
    Polley 21

Arnold, Amy 18; Betty 12; Jane
    31; Lucy 44; Martha L. 52;
    Milley 16; Patty 33; Polley 6

Atkinson, Ann 16; Median 16

Avary (Avery) Eliza 22; Elizabeth
    Maryann 47; Fanny 28; Patty
    55

Averet, Louise 32

B

B_____? Salley 54

Bain, Betsey 39

Bailey, Elizabeth 39; Jane 34;
    Martha 34; Nancy 13; Prissey
    22; Salley 6

Baker, Jincey 35; Judith 56;
    Maryanna 26; Nancy 55; Sarah
    3

Ballard, Elizabeth 39,55; Mary
    Garland 31; Rebecca 15

Baptist, Elizabeth L. 34; Mary
    35; Matilda 12

Barnes, Elizabeth 4; Rebecca 12

Barnett, Beckey 17

Barry, Margaret 24; Peggy 34

Bass, Sylvia 4

Baskervill, Ann 18; Elizabeth
    30; Mary 39; Martha 33;
    Susanna 18

Baugh, Agness 1; Elizabeth 46;
    Francis 33; Martha 23;
    Sarah 27; Tabitha 25

Beasley, Nancy 10

Beckley, Mary Anne 21

Bedingefield, Susanna 48

Benford, Polley 42; Salley 50

Bently, Ann 41

Berry, Molley 27; Sarah 23

Beville, Elizabeth 25; Martha
    55; Micah 11

Bignal, Sarah 11

Bilbo, Agnes 36; Elizabeth 7;
    Mary 36; Martha Minge 4;
    Susanna 34,46;

Billups, Lucy R. 34

Bing, Elizabeth 30; Nancy 30

Birchett, Elenor H. 47; Martha 20

Biswell, Martha 5

Bishop, Barshaba 42

Blacketter, Elizabeth B. 1;
    Keziah 29; Nancy 22; Patty
    49

Blair, Sally 9

Blake, Jinsey 1

Blanks, Dycy 22; Edna 21; Nancy
    56

Bland, Betsey 6; Fanny 27

Blankenship, Jemimah 25; Sine 54

Blackbourn, Charlotte 26; Mary
    Alford 52

Blanton, Elizabeth 48; Salley 31

Book, Hannah 3

Booker, Sarah 51

Boothe (Booth) Judith 29; Lucy
    Gilham 23; Nancy 29; Reb-
    ecca 17; Susanna 18

Boswell, Ermin 15

Bottom, Nancey 43; Sarah 31

Bowen, Caty 33; Charlotte 5;
    Judy 5; Liza 33; Nancy 44;
    Omoa 5; Rebecca 29; Stacy 9

Bowers, Milley 13

Boyd, Elizabeth 18; Jane A. 24;
    Nancey 24

Brame, Elizabeth 11,57; Elizabeth
    R. 8; Hannah C. 28; Happy
    19; Lucy 13; Mary 47;
    Susanna 6,11,33

Brawner, Mary 1

Brandon, Elizabeth 12; Nancy 20

Bradley, Elizabeth 22

Briggs, Elizabeth 14

Broadfoot, Margaret 2

Brooke, Mary 22

Brooks, Elizabeth 22,40; Jinsey
    31; Lucy 3; Molley 8;
    Nelly 29; Sarah 33

Brown, Anne 4; Catherine 2;
    Elizabeth 38; Hannah H. 33;
    Mary 49,53; Mary W. 28;
    Martha 28; Oliver 47;
    Rebecca 55; Salley 12

Brogdon, Moly Harris 19

Brooking, Lucy 25

Brummell, Polley 13

Bugg, Ann 32; Betty 26; Eliza-
    beth 1,14,21; Frances 37;
    Joyce 32; Lucy 1,19;
    Mary 53; Mary S. 53;
    Martha 39; Nancy 28; Reb-
    ecca 19; Sarah 25,31,55

Burwell, Anne Spottswood 43;
    Christian 22; Elizabeth
    Blair 49; Frances Powell
    31; Mary 45; Mary Armis-
    tead 20; Matilda 6;
    Panthea 6

Burnes, Elizabeth 8; Polly 52

Burton, Dolley 47; Frances 25;
    Mary 18,32,40; Martha 3;
    Miney 44; Peggy M. 28;
    Phebe 42,43; Susanna 16

Burrus, Amasa 44

Burrows, Elizabeth 44

Burks, Mary 53

Burnett, Elizabeth 47; Nancy 50;
    Polly Jeffries 32; Salley 5

Burchett, Elizabeth 32

Butler, Charlotte 32; Elizabeth D.
    27; Mary 4; Nancy H. 50
    Patsey 23; Sarah 29

C

Campbell, Susanna 34

Camberlaia, Elizabeth 8

Camp, Elizabeth 53; Mary 26

Carroll, Jinney 8; Judith 1; Martha
    12; Mowining 24; Nancey 51

Cardin, Jincey 51

Carter, Caty 7; Dolly 56; Judy 30;
    Letilia 17; Patsey 22; Polley
    37; Salley 13, 29

Carless, Frances 50

Carleton, Rebecca 42; Susanna 12

Cattiler, Sary 48

Chambers, Betsey 38

Chamblin, Elizabeth 38; Sarah 37

Chamblous, Mary 31

Chandler, Jean 48

Chavous (Chavis-Chavos) Anna 21;
    Elizabeth 6,45; Jiney 48; Lydia
    23; Nancy 52; Sine 52; Suckee 20

Chappell, Amey 20

Cheatham, Betsey 47; Elizabeth 55;
    Mary 15; Phebe 53; Sarah 30

Childers, Sally 17

Childress, Elizabeth 39; Jean 22

Christopher, Elizabeth 18;
    Frances 34; Hannah 32; Mary
    56; Nancy 41; Nancey 22;
    Sally 27; Susannah 39

Clark, Dianna 6; Elizabeth 26,
    32(2); Mary 14; Nancy 51;
    Sarah 18; Susanna 30

Clarke, Polly 1

Claunch, Jinny 1

Clanch, Salley 9

Clausel, Aphia W. 3; Frances
    42; Hannah H. 6; Lucey 13
    Martha 42; Salley 42

Clay, Judith 16; Patience 41;
    Prudence 32; Rebecca 18;
    Temperance 5; Temporance
    17

Clemonds, Mary 4

Cleaton, Edith 41; Elizabeth
    37; Jincey 31; Martha 57

Cole, Jincey 12

Coleman, Elizabeth 28,46;
    Elizabeth E. 38; Gracey
    25; Jane 37; Jane S. 29;
    Mary 5; Polley A. 47;
    Rebeccah 41; Salley 10

Colley, Agnes 21; Elizth: 4;
    Jane 55; Martha 1

Collier, Lucy 54; Sarah 18,
    28; Susannah B. 43

Conner, Frances 1

Cook, Elizabeth 33; Happy 49;
    Polley 37

Cooper, Nancy 1; Rebecca 10

Coppedge, Betsey 34; Susanna
    50

Corn, Hissey 49

Easter, Margaret 2; Martha 13; Sarah
56; Susanna 51

Eastland, Elizabeth 33; Mary 1

Eastham, Dicy 32

Eaton, Nancy 1; Roase 51

Edmondson (Edmundson-Edmonson) Anne
22; Elizabeth 45; Jane 53;
Martha 2; Rachel 41

Edward, Elizabeth 9

Edwards, Martha 13; Polley 2

Elam, Elizabeth 17,20; Frances 20;
Labia 21; Mary 19,33; Mary I.
23; Martha 21; Phebe 36;
Salra 48

Elliott, Jinny 8

Ellis, Patsey 14,41; Sally 47;
Sarah 19

Ellin, Nancy 24

Emery, Halley 45

Eodins, Lucy 19

Eppes (Epps) Elizabeth 37; Martha
46; Tabitha 56

Epperson, Celey 28; Claresy 55;
Elizabeth 19; Fanny 9

Erls, Nancy 21

Erskin, Mary c. 26

Evans, Catharine 43; Delilah 33;
Elizabeth 34,46; Mary 43;
Martha 18; Nancy 28;
Nanney 53; Polly 9; Prudence
33; Rebeccah 34; Salley 26

Ezell, Martha 20; Rebecca 27

Fargeson, Martha 19

Farrar, Elizabeth 18; Elliner
54; Martha 4,10; Nancy 26;
Sarah 18,52

Feagins, Lishea 41

Ferguson, Sarah 23

Ferrel, Elizabeth L. 15;
Martha 49; Sarah 54

Field (Feild) Jane 26;
Margaret 55

Finn, Jiney 5; Prudence 37;
Salley 34

Finch, Frances 40; Phebe 46;
Polley 5; Susanna 4

Floyd, Patty 40; Phebey 15

Foster, Catherine 8

Fowlks (Fowlkes) Nancy 39;
Sarah 34

Fowler, Dolly 43

Fox, Hannah 26; Mary 33;
Nancy 42; Prycillah 49
Salley 38; Sarah 56

Frazer, Elizabeth 20

Freeman, Ann 25; Anne 53;
Jane 7; Mary 51

G

Garner, Martha 17; Polley
W. 17; Susannah 25;
Winney 51

Garrott, Mary 28; Nancy 54

Gee, Lucy 15; Nancy 19

Giles, Eliza 37; Jane Perrin
3; Patsey 41

Gillispie, Susanna 26

Gillum, Martha 31

Glover, Mary 33; Salley 44

Gober, Molley 49

Gold, Elizabeth 22; Milley 50

Goodram, Nancy 55

Goodman, Susanna 6

Goodwin, Lucy 27

Goode, Elizabeth 24; Isabell 28; Janery 41; Mary 19; Nancy 26; Rebecca 46

Gordan, Ann 25; Jincey 25; Mary 51; Peggy 8

Graves, Elizabeth 20,23; Fanny W. 24; Lucretia 10; Nancy 18; Salley 48

Gregory, Anne 32; Anne C. 52; Anna 53; Elizabeth 31,48; Fanny D. 3; Frances 8; Mary 7; Mary C. 50; Martha 44; Patsey 32; Sarah 12,24; Susanna 17

Greffies, Salley 9

Greer, Jane 4

Green, Elizabeth 39; Mary 51; Patsey 24; Polley 9; Salley 19,38

Greenwood, Ann 25; Avarilla 45; Elizabeth 25; Frances 55; June 39, Mary 55; Salley 32

Grigg, Betsey 11; Patsey 37; Salley 43

Griffin, Elizabeth 48; Mary 18; Margaret 48; Nancy 15; Philadelphia 52; Susanna 21

Guy, Betsey 30; Fanney 34

Gwaltney, Susanna 46

Hailestock, Mary 50

Haile, Frances 56; Mary 9

Haley, Dosha 30

Hall, Amey 53; Anne 26; Martha B. 12; Sarah 56; Susanna 44

Hambler, Rebeccah 7

Hamblin, Elizabeth 35,51; Mary 57; Martha 29; Martha Cocke 50; Nancy 29; Phebe 17

Hanserd, Mary 41; Sarah 45

Hanvell, Martha 23

Harwell, Elizabeth P. 3

Harper, Frances 34; Martha 5

Hardy, Jane B. 17; Martha 38

Harris, Dice 1; Judith 47; Mary 20; Nanney 10; Patsey 42; Rachel 45; Salley 11,39; Susanna 23, 52

Harrison, Elith: 29; Elizabeth 46; Nancy 36; Winny 43

Haskins (Hasking) Ann N. 6; Elizabeth 11,47

Hatchell, Sally 5

Hatsel (Hatsell) Elizabeth 22; Frances 38; Polley 22; Polley Lewis 12 Salley Hunt 41

Hatch, Martha 12

Hawkins, Sarah 41

Hayes, Kitty 42; Mary 43; Nancy 52

Haywood, Penelope 55

Hendrick, Judith 39; Leah 3; Permelia B. 20; Sophia W. 56

Henly, Martha 45

Hester, Ann 42; Anna 33,36; Barbara
   6; Elizabeth 32; Henrietta 21;
   Jane 6,34; Lilly 6; Lively 15;
   Lucy 7; Mary 8,36; Martha 39

Hetton, Prudence 24

Hicks (Hix) Duamar 2

Hightower, Sarah 4

Hill, Phebe 24

Hinton, Mary 41; Nancy 40

Hix (Hicks) Elizabeth 25; Lucy 7

Hoard, Fanney 35

Hobson, Agnes 17

Hogan, Ann 28; Ede 17; Mary 17;
   Prudence 45

Hollins, Caty 1

Holloway, Dianna 12; Elizabeth 18,
   50; Lucy 56; Martha 3; Nancy
   55; Patsy 27; Salley 35

Holmes, Ann 27,54; Betsey 54;
   Elizabeth 14,29; Fanney 7;
   Faithy 47; Frances 54; Joice
   20; Lucy 49; Lucinda 54; Mary
   16,52; Mary A. 17; Martha 1;
   Patty 32; Polly 3; Rebecca
   43; Salley 43,57; Sarah 15;
   Susannah 3

Hood, Keziah 16

Hopkins, Elizabeth 14, Jane 42

House, Nancy 13

Howard, Martha 37

Hubbard, Patsey 47

Hudgins, Dolley 16; Elizabeth
   F. 44

Hudson, Betty 27; Chary 23;
   Dicy 1; Elizabeth 1,8,55;
   Judith 42; Lucy 19,40;
   Margary 13; Nancy 9; Polly
   42; Sarah 36; Susanna 43

Humphress, Stacy 2

Humphries, Martha 8; Monier 7;
   Nancy 35

Hunt, Ann 29; Elizabeth 20;
   Lockey 9; Mary Ann 24;
   Nancy 18

Hunley (Hundley) Lucy 51;
   Nancy 48; Polley 17

Hurt, Patience 17

Hutson, Sarah 7

Hutt (Hut) Jincey 25; Mary
   43; Nancy 13; Pettey 44;
   Salley 12;

Hutcheson, Anna 6; Elizabeth
   4,17,39,48; Fanny 27;
   Frances C. 8; Hannah 36;
   Lucy 46; Mary 51; Martha
   41; Polley 29; Salley 7;
   Sarah 27; Susanna 25,48

Hyde, Elinor 47; Martha 56;
   Sarah 16

I

Inge, Sally 11

Ingram, Lucy 43; Lucy Worsham
   8; Tabitha 50

Insco, Jinny 10; Martha N. 4

J

Jackson, Betsey Ann 30; Cha-
   rity 30; Elizabeth 18;
   Jemimah 31; Mourning 53;
   Nancy 50; Prudence 10

Salley 4; Sarah 29; Tellathacum 51

James, Mary 53

Jeffries, Ann 38; Elizabeth 8,39; Elizth: 28; Jane 3,38; Martha 8,17; Nancy 19; Polly Cluverias 7; Sarah 7; Susannah 25; Susannah B. 13

Jeffress, Lucy 7

Johnson, Betsey 14; Caty 10; Jane 36; Leannah 17; Lucy 40; Martha 34; Nancy 15;16; Rebecca 14; Sarah 28

Johnston, Elizabeth 8; Sally 2

Jones, Caty 20; Easter 13; Elizth: 10; Elizabeth 32,46; Johanna 48; Little 32; Lucy 10; Lacy Green 24; Mary 20,40; Martha 10,15,46; Martha Cary 26; Patty 35; Polly 3; Putres 50; Rebecca 4; Sarah Anderson 6; Tabitha 7

Jordan, Elizabeth 21; Mary W. 21; Martha W. 35

K

Keeton, Aubrey 45; Elizabeth 10, 27; Mary 27; Nancy 4

Kelley, Elizabeth 51; Nancy 51

King, Edith 24; Frances 38

Kendrick, Sarah 40

Kirks, Amey 35; Betsey S. 5; Patty 52

Kirkland, Anne 11; Sarah 17

Knight, Sarah 44

Knott, Frankey 57

Ladd, Henrietter 24; Huldy 36

Laffoon, Patsy 50

Lamb, Mary E. 44

Lambert, Biddy 23; Judith 43; Lemenda 36; Mary 20; Milly 8; Mourning 49; Sibbe 47

Langford, Elizabeth 56

Lanier, Betsey 18; Nancy 4; Patty 18; Polley 30; Tabitha 4

Lark, Ann 12; Elizabeth 54; Joice 49; Morning 46; Salley 50

Lavingston, Catherine 54

Leagon, Annis 28

Leach, Martha 50

Leigh, Aryness 9

Lett, Frances 39; Leliah 37; Patsey 46; Polley 15; Suckey Burrus 32

Lewis, Ann 52; Elzh: 7; Elizabeth 39; Mary 5; Martha 52; Nancy 1

Lidderdil, Sarah 36

Loafman, Prudence 27

Lockett (Locket) Anne 20; Elizabeth 5; Lucy 30; Nancy 25; Phebe 40

Love, Agniss 44

Lowry, Polley 19

Lowberry, Lucy 34

Lowance, Margaret 42

Loyd, Celia 37; Martha 13; Rebekah 13

Lucas, Ann 16; Elizabeth 15; Frances
25; Sarah 39; Susanna P. 40

Lunsford, Polly 17

M

McDaniel, Lucy 49

McGuire (see McQuire)

McHarg, Elizabeth Q. 1; Mary Watts
24

McKinney, Jinney 14

McLaughlin, Elizabeth 45

McLin, Fanny 9; Mary 52

McQuire, Jincy 56

Mabry, Elizabeth 5; Polley 40

Malone _____? 36; Betsey 45; Lizzy
46; Lucy 11; Patsey 21; Phebe
56; Salley 37; Sophia 22

Manning, Polley 48

Marshall, Alice 14; Ann 51; Betsey
Green 29; Elizabeth 25,42;
Mary Ann 4; Martha Goode 32;
Phibby A. 12; Salley 14;
Salley Read 5; Susanna 3,22

Marine, Henryetta 18

Marks, Nancy 35

Massey, Mary 3; Patsey 17

Mason, Lucy 30; Milley 17; Nancy
51; Patsy 13; Rebecca 43;
Rody 33

Matthews, Elizabeth 12; Martha 36,
47; Nancy 40; Sarah 23

May, Siller 44

Mayo, Elizabeth 17

Mayes, Elizabeth 22

Mayne, Mary M. 11; Parmelia 29;
Patsey M. 31

Maynard, Frances 4; Judith 20;
Mary 56

Mealer, Betsey 47; Frances 42;
Martha 42; Polley 53; Susanna 42

Medley, Lucy 18

Merriott, Constant 1

Merryman, Polly 31; Salley 3

Merrymoon, Betsy 52

Michaux, Lucy 56

Mills, Amey 56; Nancy 54

Minor, Patsy 13; Sarah 28

Mitchell, Nancy 6; Patsey 8;
Rebeccah 7

Monroe, Polley 14

Moore, Betsey 30; Elizabeth
38; Lucy 55; Mary Anne
45; Mary 14; Martha 20;
Phebe 55; Polley 55;
Rebecah 51; Taffanus 27

Moody, Elizabeth 36; Mary
14; Nancy 21; Phebe 49;
Polley 36

Morgan, Betsey 43; Edith 43;
Mary 29; Molley 43;
Patsey 33; Polly H. 43;
Sarah 31,38

Morgain, Nancy 1

Morris, Polley 45

Moss, Elizabeth 11; Fanny 27;
Lucy 42; Martha 39; Patsy
38

Mosely, Milly 42

Mullins, Betsey 27; Lucy 43; Mary 14, 43; Salley 10; Susannah 23

Munford, Elizabeth Beverley 30

Murfey, Nancy 4

Murdock, Seller 46

Murray, Ann Bolling 7; Elizabeth 57; Susanna 45

N

Naish (Nash) Jinney 9; Judith 36; Lucy 55; Nancy 56; Sarah 13

Nance, Elizabeth 36; Judith 1; Molley 1; Tabitha 33

Nanney (Nanny) Patsey 56; Tempy 47; William 30

Neal, Elizabeth 6; Mary 35; Nancy 13; Polly 35

Nelson, Lucy 38; Nancy Carter 30

Newton, Elizabeth 38; Milley 56

Nicholson, Mary 4

Nicholas, Ann 21

Nolley, Rebecca 23

Norman, Mary 6

Northington, Betsey Edwards 36; Elizabeth 32; Sarah 10

Norment, Frances 27; Janey 17; Nancy 47

Norvell, Martha 19

Nuckalls, Ann 54

Nunnelly, Polley 14

Nunnery, Salley 51; Susanna 50

O

Oliver, Elizabeth 8,31; Frances 8

Ornsby, Ellender 10

Osling (Oslin) Elizabeth 4; Nancy 37; Polley 47; Rebecca 57

Overby (Overbey) Elizabeth 17; Liddy 34; Meloda 53; Nancy D. 5

Overton, Elizabeth 42; Salley 27; Susannah 11,53

P

Page, Betsey 42; Caty 47

Palmer, Mary 9; Nancy 57

Parham, Ann 31; Lelilah 23; Mary 7

Parsons, Elizabeth 9

Parrett, Martha C. 49

Parrish, Mary 51

Pattillo, Rebecca 6

Pearry Nancy 5

Pearce (Peirce) Lucy 48

Pennington, Ann 36,39; Anne 38; Elizabeth 15; Frances 32; Fatha 31; Janney 12; Lucy 47; Mary N. 23; Martha 23; Polly 54; Tabitha 37; Tokey 38

Person, Elizabeth 1

Persize, Mary 31

Pettus, Amey 49; Elizabeth Walker 40; Elizabeth 45; Harriott 30; Mary 40; Martha 12; Sarah 29; Susanna 5,40

Rubards, Phebe 43

Rudd, Martha 39; Nancy 47; Sally 22;
Salley 26

Ruffin, Martha 38

Russell, Elizabeth 29; Jane Wright
47; Mary 14; Martha 53; Milley
8; Patsy 13; Prudence 28; Sarah
37; Salley 29

Ryland, Jiney J. 8

S

Salley (Sally) Happy 34; Mary 50;
Magdala 5

Sanders, Jane 21; Mary 55

Saunders, Elizabeth 52; Milly 56;
Nancy 37; Ora 16

Scott, Mira Parson 29; Pheby 9

Seward, Creasy 26

Short, Caty Humphries 9; Eddy 51;
Elizabeth 14; Elizabeth H. 53;
Janey 18; Mary T. 48; Martha
14; Nancy 16; Polley 26;
Rebecca J. 53; Salley 26

Simmons, Catherine 16; Lucy 5;
Martha 44

Singleton, Mary 50; Nancy 16

Skelton, Patsey 1

Skipwith, Helen 11

Skinner, Elizabeth 22

Small, Mary 10

Smith, Aggy 24; Ann 52; Elizabeth
28,35,55; Lucy 20; Mary 9,19;
Martha 17; Nancy 47,49;
Peggy 3; Polley 54; Pricilla
12; Sarah 1,51; Susanna 12,
20,22,47

Spain, Judy 52; Polly 2

Sparks, Martha 5

Speed, Elizabeth I. 49; Lucy
29; Mary 16; Martha 2,37;
Nancy 40; Sarah 7,16,23

Spurlock, Aggy 33; Milley 51

Stainback, James 37; Jean 16;
Martha Johnson 31; Polley
29

Standley, Ann 43; Lucy 20;
Mary 57

Starling, Ann 26

Stevens, Polly 9

Stembridge, Polley 43

Stewart (Stuart) Amy 17;
Betsey 53; Celey 35;
Eliza 48; Elizabeth 38;
Lina 10; Lucy 50; Mary 11;
Mahala 46; Milley 53; Nan-
ey 16; Nancy 47; Polly 22;
Prissey 28; Precilla 49;
Rebecca 9; Rittah 23;
Salley 35; Thurdy 50

Stigall (Steagall-Stegall)
Elizabeth 37; Mary 10;
Martha 18

Stokes, Mary M. 11

Stone, Catherine 45; Hannah 55;
Mary 35; Nancy 8,27;
Polley 50; Salley 53;
Susa 18

Suggett, Elizabeth 35; Lucy
41; Molley 27

Sullevant, Mary 24

Swepson, Jane 57; Lucy 47;
Sarah 46; Susanna 15

Tabb, Elizabeth 3; Mary 49; Margaret
   30

Tain, Patty 54

Talley, Mary Anne 13; Patsey 15

Tanner, Delina 45; Mary 18,26; Mary
   Ann 4; Rebecca 41; Sarah 4

Tarry, Mary 13

Taylor, Betsey 16; Elizabeth 56;
   Joyce Lark 27; Judith 21;
   Lucy 11; Mary 6,26,45; Mary
   C. 7; Martha 11,45; Penelope
   12,34; Polley Jones 54;
   Rebecca B. 41; Rebeccah 51;
   Sarah 14,31,49; Sally 16;
   Susanna 54

Thornton, Jane 25; Salley 2

Thompson, Elizabeth 32$^{(2)}$,51;
   Judith 47; Letty 17; Martha
   15; Molley 50; Nancey 25; Nancy 13,28; Patsey 3; Polley
   4; Rebekah 4; Sarah 50

Thomason, Judith 3; Polley 46;
   Suckey 9

Thomerson, Elizabeth 35; Sally
   56

Thomas, Nanny 40; Nancy 23,44

Tibbs, Sarah 35

Tindal, Polley 21

Tisdale, Beckey 46; Levina 11;
   Phebe 50

Toone, Martha 39; Polley 53; Sarah
   10;

Tucker, Amy 13; Catherine 12,51;
   Elizabeth 13; Frances 51;
   Jane 51; Lucy 27; Mary 30;
   Mary Thweate 7; Polley 30

Turner, Betsey 41; Lucretia 35;
   Mary 43; Milley 26;Nancy 28,53

Polley 28; Salley 27;
   Wilmouth 28

U

Underwood, Levina 54; Willey 21

V

Valentine, Lucy 45

Varnel, Sally 9

Vaughan, Clary 8; Elizabeth 3,
   6,48,55; Ermen 27; Fanny
   42; Frances 38; Hannah
   52; Jane 14; Martha 26,
   28; Nancy 10,36,53;
   Patsey 7,36; Rebecca 4;
   Rody 38

Venable, Anne 33

W

Wade, Isabella 51; Margaret 23
   Polly 47; Sarah 27

Wadkins, Mary 50

Wagstaff, Elzth: 15; Lilley 27;
   Mary 16; Polly 27; Salley
   35

Walton, Anne 28

Walden, Mary H. 54; Polley 49;
   Siller 48; Tabitha 7

Walker, Agga 19; Agnes 34;
   Ann E. 10; Elizabeth 13,
   17; Fanney 41; Jean 18;
   Mary 47; Phebee 46;
   Polley 17; Salley 12;
   Sally H. 52; Tabitha 6

Wall, Caty 10,16; Rebecka 24;.
   Salley 24

Waller, Caty 55; Lucy 24; Nancy 10

Warren, Elizabeth 36; Polley
   19

Watts, Elizabeth Hanner Barbary 2;
Frances Anne 50

Watson, Charlotte 3; Martha 46;
Rebeccah 1; Rebecca 15;
Tabitha 44

Weatherford, Amy 54; Sarah 47

Weakes, Frances 12

Webb, Leannah Basey 28; Nancy 11;
Tabitha 23

Weight, Jane 41; Martha 52; Sarah
L. 11

Wells, Anne 42; Hannah 34

Westmoreland, Mary 20

Westbrook, Phoebe 24

White, Elizabeth 15; Elanner 35;
Jincy 15; Mary 3,18,23;
Nancy 27

Whitehead, Elizabeth 10,49; Jane
28; Nancy 19; Sarah 11

Whitlow, Anne 20

Whilbey, Elizabeth Hill 24

Whoberry (Whobry) Molley 22;
Nancy 8; Sally 5

Williams, Darcus 5; Jane 36; Martha
21; Nancy 4; Obedience 12;
Patsey 37; Sarah Osling 15;
Salley 27

Williamson, Elizabeth 41; Jincey 3;
Nancy 10

Wilson, Ann 10; Elizabeth 10,42;
Francis 31; Lucy 34; Mary 23;
47; Nancy 22; Susanna 54;
Tabitha 47.

Wiles, Temple 14

Wilkerson, Agness 57; Betsey 35

Wilborn (Wilburn),Elizabeth 53;
Nancey 25

Willis,Elizabeth 49; Mary 22;
Nancy 32

Winn (see Wynn)

Winkler, Charlotte 54

Winkfield, Rebecca 3

Winfield, Dolley 53; Mary 44;
Martha 44; Nancy 30

Wootton, Barbary 3; Elizabeth
14

Worsham, Elizabeth 25,38; Polly
2; Rebecca 2; Salley 57

Wray, Sarah 39

Wright, Elizabeth 30; Mary 26;
Nancy 15,19,56,57; Polly
16; Sally 13

Wynn (Winn) Elizth: 34; Frances
37; Jane 55; Kitty 2;
Nancy 54

Y

Yancey, Delphia 51; Elizabeth
21; Mary 56; Nancy 21;
Polley 33; Susanna 39,56

Yates, Milley 50

Yeargen, Elizabeth 36; Nancy
36

Young, Elanor 44; Judith B.
32; Lucy 32; Mary 49
Susannah 49

----

www.ingramcontent.com/pod-product-compliance
Lightning Source LLC
Chambersburg PA
CBHW071233290326
41931CB00037B/2897